Praise for *The Complete 4 for Literacy*

"Teachers who are looking for help designing their reading and writing curriculums will find a new best friend in Pam Allyn. This wise, thoughtful, and practical book will help them put the pieces of the literacy puzzle together to create a perfect year for students."

—CARL ANDERSON, author of *How's It Going?*
and *Assessing Writers*

"Pam reminds us of the power of reading aloud, the magical pull the music of language can have on the human spirit. She reminds us of the influence a single teacher can have, an influence that can ripple out across decades and countless lives. She reminds us that, as teachers, we have knowledge that sets us apart from the general public and that knowledge can and should be the guiding force in our teaching. And she reminds us to always, always temper that knowledge with our common sense."

—LESTER LAMINACK, author of *Cracking Open Craft* and *Learning Under the Influence of Language and Literature*

"Pam Allyn's *The Complete 4 for Literacy* is essential reading for teachers who want to rethink and deepen their reading and writing year."

—GEORGIA HEARD, author of *The Revision Toolbox* and *Writing Toward Home*

"I love this book and so will every teacher who seeks a "systematic approach that allows for flexibility and teacher preference." Imagine, a complete learning plan, not only for your grade, but for all grade levels. This will change the nature of how you think about instruction and long range planning. I COMPLETELY recommend The Complete 4 for Literacy and applaud this grand accomplishment."

—JUDY DAVIS, author of *The No Nonsense Guide to Teaching Writing: Strategies, Structures, Solutions*

"This wise and wonderful book invites teachers to live toward a perfect year of teaching. Pam Allyn's humor and long, rich teaching experience are woven into the work she describes here: teaching young writers to love reading and writing, to be independent, to have stamina, and to make good choices. Using her "Complete 4" framework—process, genre, strategy, and conventions—will help teachers design units and individual lessons that are robust and meaningful. A must have for teachers!"

—JANET ANGELILLO, author of *Making Revision Matter* and *A Fresh Approach to Teaching Punctuation*

"This is a journey every school must undertake if it wants to cultivate a skillful and knowledgeable staff. Pam Allyn shows us the way, helping us learn to be precise and deliberate about every step we take."

—EMMA SUÁREZ-BÁEZ, Literacy Coordinator and Coach, P.S. 340 Bronx, N.Y.

"At last, a flexible framework that respects teachers and believes in their ability to make good, instructional decisions! The Complete 4 recognizes that in the area of curriculum planning "one size does not fit all" and offers a comprehensive guide to developing a balanced, quality reading and writing curriculum."

—JANET KNIGHT, Kindergarten Teacher, Mamaroneck, NY

"Finally a balance. . . . *The Complete 4 for Literacy* is a must read for all educators who aim to organize their teaching of reading and writing into thoughtful units, while at the same time, utilizing their students as their number one curriculum informants. Pam's framework will encourage professional conversation among all school staff members. . . . conversation about thoughtful literacy instruction across grades, a balanced curriculum that allows for differentiation, and at the heart, the importance of joyful teaching."

—JOANNE HINDLEY, author of *In the Company of Children*

Pam Allyn

The Complete 4 for Literacy

PROCESS
GENRE
STRATEGY
CONVENTIONS

How to Teach Reading and Writing Through Daily Lessons, Monthly Units, and Yearlong Calendars

■ SCHOLASTIC

NEW YORK • TORONTO • LONDON • AUCKLAND • SYDNEY
MEXICO CITY • NEW DELHI • HONG KONG • BUENOS AIRES

Cover design by Jay Namerow

Interior design by Maria Lilja

Interior photos by Maria Lilja unless otherwise indicated

Acquiring Editor: Lois Bridges

Production Editor: Erin Kathleen Liedel

Copy Editor: Shelley Griffin

ISBN 13: 978-0-439-02644-4

ISBN 10: 0-439-02644-X

Copyright © 2007 by Pam Allyn

To all teachers, who are so dedicated to the lives of children,
and with love to my own first lifelong teachers:
my parents, Anne and Bill Krupman

Table of Contents

Acknowledgments

I love communities. I love creating and being created by circles of people united together around common goals and shared dreams. I am lucky to have many connected communities in my life. These words are dedicated to them.

My deep appreciation goes to the LitLife community. Composed of my extraordinary team of colleagues, office staff, and interns, you work so hard on behalf of LitLife and on behalf of the power of this work to change lives. I appreciate all you do.

Some of my colleagues have given their invaluable assistance to bringing this book to life: Patty Vitale-Reilly, executive director of LitLife West Hudson, both a great business partner and rock of my life; Laurie Pastore, whose luminous wisdom, generosity, and values inspire me; Karen McNally, who infuses every

conversation about this work and life with care and thoughtfulness; Abi Gotthelf, whose sharp eye focuses us when we most need it; and Jaime Margolies, a magnificent teacher who shows me that joy and academic rigor can both have a home in the same room.

The LitLife community includes our spectacular schools, clients extraordinaire: teachers, administrators, office staff, parents, and, of course, the blessed children with whom we work. Thank you for opening your doors to us and trying out our new ideas. A special thanks to Sonja Cherry-Paul, Janet Knight, Valerie Palacio and their marvelous students.

I spent a decade at The Columbia University Reading and Writing Project. I give thanks for Lucy Calkins, my first mentor and my lifelong friend, and all the great teacher leaders I met there, especially Nick Flynn, Carl Anderson, Georgia Heard, and Rory Freed. In addition, I thank my wonderful longtime friends and colleagues Joanne Hindley and Judy Davis. I met Naomi Nye in those years, and she continues to inspire me with her life and her work to this day.

I spend as much of my "spare" time as I can at The Children's Village, where I lead an initiative called Books for Boys. The children of New York's foster care system have been my great teachers, too. I believe that everything I say about this work should apply to all children; the Village is my essential touchstone. To the spectacular women who lead this initiative with me, my thanks and love: Susan Meigs, Elizabeth Fernandez, Nancy Kliot, Joanne Levine, Lauren Blum, Erica Mason, and Lori McFarlane. Equally, my thanks go to the dedicated staff at The Children's Village.

The community of Scholastic has been so supportive and has believed in *The Complete 4* from the first. Thanks to all the members of the team—Gloria Pipkin, Amy Rowe, Ray Coutu, Erin Kathleen Liedel, Maria Lilja—and especially Terry Cooper and Jaime Lucero, who have such an extraordinary commitment to excellence in educational publishing.

My daughter said to me recently how lucky I am that I found an editor who is not only funny and wise, but who also has become a true friend. How right she is. I am grateful today and always for the rare combination of genius and humanity of Lois Bridges.

To my communities of friends near and far, thank you for so much joy. A special thanks to Jeannie Blaustein, Peter Bokor, and their daughters Sophie and Livia for their multitude of talents and kindnesses and for showing us what friendship is all about.

My family circle is the essential community, with thanks to my relatives who create that circle. All my gratitude to my parents, Anne and Bill Krupman, and my in-laws, Cindy and Louis Allyn, who are the staunchest supporters of the LitLife dream. They are wonderful parents and grandparents too. My heartfelt appreciation to "Aunt" Rita Phillips, who has given her time to our annual LitLife events and is beloved by our LitLife team.

To the community of my heart: our beautiful daughters, Katie and Charlotte, who not only let me come into their classrooms from the time they were in nursery school and "practice" all my new teaching ideas with them, but who also give us the best business advice (seriously). Thank you for all the fun we have together and for the extraordinary young women you are. I am so proud of you.

Aunt Alice said "Marry someone who is funny." My mother said "Marry someone who is nice to children." My father said "Marry someone who is smart." Luckily for me, I found the person who is all of those things and more. To the great, incomparable, one and only Jim Allyn—my business partner, my life partner, my best, best friend, my compatriot in all aspects of this life large and small—you complete me.

Pam Allyn
April 2007

Introduction

This is actually my second book. My first I wrote when I was 8 years old in third grade. My teacher was Mrs. Kovacs. At the time, I knew right away that I had found my kindred spirit and my hero. She was warm, kind, joyous, generous, wise. She was very young. My mother recalls that it was probably only her third year of teaching. Looking back, I realize now she was an innovator. She instinctively knew how to create a classroom where literacy was not just instruction; it was sheer and utter pleasure.

She differentiated instruction long before that approach was widely practiced. Every single child was known to her because every single day she had what she called "small talks" with each of us. These days we would call them conferences. No one taught her to do this. She just clearly knew that she wanted to get to know her students, and we could feel it every minute of every day. Her common sense and her strong belief that children thrive on both freedom and structure led her to create many opportunities for us to work on our own projects, even at such a young age. With the space to think, the room to grow, and her championing of all of our sometimes eccentric but always interesting ideas, I remember very vividly that each of us pursued passions, topics, and ideas that might not always have been brilliant, but which we nevertheless found endlessly interesting.

In her classroom, I woke up to the sound of literature. She read aloud to us from all the books she had loved as a child. She told us how her mother had read to her. She read to us from books and poems that were well above our "reading levels." So this was where I penned the opus *Thunder: A Horse*. To be honest, it was a thinly veiled "retelling" of an abridged version of *Black Beauty*. Names were changed, the horse was "dappled" (because I loved that word), not black, and since I loved the beginning of that abridged version of *Black Beauty*, I began my own tome with the line, "Under an apple tree, a foal was born."

I could not get over this line, lifted directly from that edition of *Black Beauty*. It was magic to me. I repeated it to myself each day on my way to school. It didn't start like so many other stories did, with "Once there was..." It wasn't rigidly controlled vocabulary like so many of the texts we were reading during other times of the day and that I had read the year before in the first and second grades.

The sentence was complex, rhythmic, and visual. In short, it was the perfect sentence.

The first time I had heard it was when Mrs. Kovacs read it aloud to us in one of our many read-aloud sessions with her. When she saw the finished draft of my masterpiece, she smiled at that first line and whispered to me, "I have always loved that line too." She was a magnificent teacher. I was very shy; I hardly ever talked in school although I had plenty to say at home with my parents. She was the first person outside my family to give great dignity to what I was thinking about and feeling. I will be forever indebted to her for this.

About eight years ago, I called the school system in which I had lived at the time to see if I could find her. The district secretary was kind enough to do a little research. She called me back a few days later, and there was a catch in her voice. She said, "I am really sorry to tell you this. But what I found out was that Mrs. Kovacs died in a car accident a few years ago." Mrs. Kovacs had moved soon after I had had her as my teacher. The district

secretary also told me that, in an amazing coincidence, someone else, a man, had called the district office asking about Mrs. Kovacs right after I had called. The secretary told me, "The length of time she taught here was so brief that the person who called must have been a peer of yours."

Imagine that 35 years later, at least two people in the world continue to feel completely changed by their third-grade teacher. I wonder if he too remembered Mrs. Kovacs's "small talks" and the sound of her voice on a January winter day, leaning into us, saying, "Under an apple tree, a foal was born."

I am really grateful to all teachers who, like Mrs. Kovacs, see teaching not just as a profession, but in truth as a kind of a calling. A call to words, to human connectedness, and to dignifying the lives of children.

This book is for you.

PART ONE

The Complete Year

In the great classic *Mary Poppins*, P. L. Travers uses a very interesting technique to identify moments of importance, especially those that might seem less important on the surface. She capitalized not just big moments such as Her Day Out, but small details, as in "Miss Lark lived Next Door." Mary Poppins was able to talk to animals and babies. Magically, she could understand their responses.

Mary Poppins is quite structured and believes deeply in conventions, everything from the importance of capital letters to the starch in her dress, but she is also the person who takes Jane and Michael on their greatest adventures. When they and Mary Poppins find themselves in the zoo with the animals after hours, they spin a compass and are magically able to go around the world.

Mary Poppins knew what to emphasize. She knew how to listen to the language of babies and animals. She knew what composed a good adventure.

And she knew when to capitalize.

We all strive for completeness, when we reach a fullness and a richness in our own lives and our own teaching, and when what we are doing may be remembered well enough to deserve its own capital letters.

Mary Poppins most certainly knew the value of conventions, but she was not afraid to take a risk. Part One of this book is designed to introduce you to the flexible framework that will help you build a complete year, with both convention (order and structure) and the processes of learning—and the adventure that comes from creating together.

What do we mean by a "complete year"? One in which everything works perfectly? In which every teaching moment resonates with our students, sticks with them, and is evident in their reading and writing the very next day?

That is not the nature of life nor is it the nature of teaching! To me, a complete year in the teaching of reading and writing is one in which my teaching is thoughtful and prepared, spontaneous and joyous. Where the journey is always exciting—even when I hit bumps—and where, at the end of the year, I bid farewell to my students, knowing they will soon join a new teacher who will guide them through the next phase of their educational journey.

Part One introduces you to a systematic approach for planning and implementing reading and writing instruction. It will balance your instruction across the year, addressing the teaching as four key components: a knowledge of genre, an awareness of and application of strategy, the development of good reading and writing habits, and a growing understanding of how to use conventions effectively. Additionally, Part One will show you how to teach units of study with specific focus and standards-based outcomes across the year. Part One will also introduce developmental continua to enable you to plan instruction and curriculum that aligns with the unique needs of your own students.

CHAPTER 1

Welcome to The Complete 4

You love kids, you love teaching, and you love teaching kids to read and write. You often think about how to teach even more effectively; you talk with colleagues; you read professional literature. And still your teaching does not feel quite right. Life may be about using time wisely, and the pressure of time is felt so intensely in the classroom. There is simply not enough time. Not enough time to plan, not enough time to teach, not enough time to assess. Even to the most confident and experienced practitioners, the teaching of reading and writing can feel like a giant juggling act.

And despite the fact that every classroom has its own unique kids and its own unique culture, increased accountability pressures force you to accept a one-size-fits-all curriculum. You may sometimes feel constrained by state and federal mandates, curriculum requirements and maps, district programs and materials, required assessments and tests. Your world is one of limited freedom and many dictated practices.

On the other hand, your time with your students is yours to make of it what you will. How will you create a community of trust and respect, of fun and excitement, of enthusiasm for learning? How will you fashion the particular lesson you want to teach that day on author's craft? How will your students learn the basics of punctuation and grammar? How will your lesson provide a practical teaching point while extending students' understanding of the glorious potential of literacy, slowly and surely turning them into proficient, curious readers and writers?

This time when you can personalize and individualize your teaching is when you're able to act as a professional decision maker and experience the joy inherent in teaching. This time in your classroom when you begin your lesson, when you have the resources and the confidence and the support of colleagues and administration, is the most exciting time of the day.

I believe that teachers experience a great deal of unnecessary stress and anxiety when they encounter these twin perils—too much of their teaching practice is dictated and too little support is given during the times they are engaging in the essential creation and implementation of lessons in the classroom. This tension in the world of teaching—between systemic mandates limiting my flexibility in the classroom and not enough support for my own Independent Practice—is one that I felt the first time I set foot in a classroom as a teacher, and is a constant refrain in my work with teachers at all grade levels. You don't want to be forced to operate in a rigid structure, and you also don't want to have the burdensome feeling of going it alone in your teaching.

Teachers want a flexible framework.

Celebrate Flexibility: You Are in Charge!

You want flexibility: a guide to teaching that gives the comfortable support of well thought-out plans and structures for your teaching; a plan in which a lot of the heavy lifting is already done; a plan you can easily modify to accommodate the "must haves" and the "must dos" but still teach the units and lessons you want to teach.

And you want a framework: lessons and units of study that give a coherence to your teaching throughout the day, the month, and the year. You need ideas and content to use in your teaching, right at your fingertips, awaiting your own tweaking and modifying so they become your own and you feel comfortable and at home in your teaching.

The Complete 4 is the flexible framework you need.

It answers the simple question, "Why can't we have it all?" with the heartfelt belief that you *can* have it all in your teaching life. My colleagues wanted me to title this book *A Perfect Year of Teaching Reading and Writing*. We all want perfect years, and not just in our teaching. And while I truly love the life I am leading and I love teaching children, I have certainly never had a perfect year. But the hope of having one, and the understanding that it is the striving for perfection that makes so many good things happen, makes every day burst with opportunity. This book gives you the tools to make every teaching day more enjoyable and your teaching more powerful, and enhances the promise of having a perfect year.

Maximize Your Teaching Time: Integrate Reading and Writing

Reading is comprehension; writing is composition. Yet both involve processing language to affect (and effect) understanding in the world. In reading we gain an understanding of the world *from* someone else; in writing we set forth an understanding of the world *to* someone else. And reading and writing are fundamentally united with each other. As I read, I am surrounded by the rhythm of the words, the flow of the story, the dramatic turn of events. And I can use all that knowledge, all those sensations, when I write and send my story out into the world.

My essential point here is that the teaching of reading and writing should be unified to the greatest extent possible. Doing so not only makes sense pedagogically, but it actually simplifies your teaching practice. Not only does integrating reading and writing maximize learning, but it also gives you more of what all teachers crave—time. This idea, which has been field-tested by teachers and vetted by administrators, powerfully impacts every aspect of school life—from the daily classroom lesson to the broadest brushes of curriculum planning across grade levels. It is called The Complete 4. The Complete 4 guide will show you how to join the teaching of reading and writing wherever possible. A Complete 4 teacher considers balance all through the year, and has a system and a plan for ensuring a healthy mix in her teaching of reading and writing across the year. When I ask teachers what they think are important outcomes for students as readers and writers, they will often say the following:

- Learning to love reading and writing

- Achieving independence in reading and writing

- Developing stamina

- Making good choices for books and topics

Let me now show you how The Complete 4 promotes those values.

Profound Understandings That Inform The Complete 4

If you were to identify the qualities of the strong, effective readers and writers you admire, your list would likely include the following:

Knowledge and Understanding of the Reading and Writing Process

Effective readers and writers:

- Understand themselves as readers and writers

- Choose texts and topics to match their purpose

- Have excellent stamina in reading through texts and writing on the page

- Read and write with fluency

- Talk about and generate ideas with others

- Use tools in a way that deepens their thinking

Knowledge and Understanding of the Variety of Genres

Effective readers and writers:

- Anticipate consistent structures as they read or write in a particular genre

- Approach a text with a mindset that corresponds to the specific genre

- Approach the blank page and select a genre that aligns with their purpose for reading or writing

Knowledge and Understanding of Reading and Writing Strategies

Effective readers and writers:

- Apply reading decoding and comprehension strategies to deepen understanding of text

- Apply writing strategies both to the blank page and to drafts already in progress

- Are metacognitive about how they approach difficult texts or challenges in their writing, meaning they exercise active control over the process of thinking that is used in learning situations (Metacognitive skills are those such as planning how one will approach a learning task, self-monitoring comprehension, and being able to assess how much progress is being made toward achieving the goal.)

- Use organizational structures to develop a sense of the meaning of what they are reading and to build clarity in what they are writing about

Knowledge and Understanding of Standard English Conventions

Effective readers and writers:

- Have a strong awareness of grammatically correct structures

- Use punctuation to read smoothly and confidently and to write clearly

- Choose words carefully

- Craft sentences and paragraphs that best convey the intended meaning

Given these characteristics of good readers and writers, the question then becomes, "How can I design and put into practice teaching methods in my classroom that will maximize my students' development of these traits throughout the year?"

As with almost all successful ventures, both planning and execution are the keys to success. Designing our year with conscious attention to the ultimate skills we want to impart to our students forces us to create a thoughtful structure for our teaching of reading and writing. The Complete 4 serves the twin purposes of focusing your thinking during the planning stage, and easing your actual in-class implementation of the plan.

Simplify and Structure: How The Complete 4 Helps

The Complete 4 is a response to the need we all have as teachers to frame our thinking. Because the balance between reading and writing is difficult to precisely quantify in teaching practice, I have identified four different components that will help us clarify the what, why, when, and how of our teaching (see Chapter 2 for a thorough overview of each component).

The Complete 4

The Complete 4 provides a framework within which to guide our teaching, while recognizing the inherent fluidity of teaching reading and writing. Its four components are process, genre, strategy, and conventions. Thoughtfully integrating these components into our teaching leads to a beautifully blended year of literacy instruction.

- **Process**

  The process component is the foundation of instruction, ensuring that students have the tools and skills they need to thrive as readers and writers, across genres and across disciplines. Process has to do with developing a sense of self as a reader and writer, the habits of mind students develop as readers and writers (how does each individual student approach reading and writing?), and the personal and classroom routines that enable the development of successful reading and writing habits.

- **Genre**

  We read and write for multiple purposes and in multiple forms. Genre can be thought of as a "container for thought" that reflects both purpose and form. In The Complete 4 we study narrative, poetry, nonfiction, and standardized tests.

- **Strategy**

  The strategy component has to do with the techniques and skills we can explicitly teach our students in their reading and writing that transcend a particular genre or assignment. Such strategic thinking and action promote fluency and comprehension in reading, and effectiveness and eloquence in writing, whatever the genre or particular assignment.

- **Conventions (grammar and punctuation)**

  The conventions component gives students a deep-rooted understanding of the formalities and accepted structures of reading and writing within the different genres. These are the understandings about syntax, punctuation, parts of speech, and word study that enable effective reading and writing.

Integrating these four components in a balanced and considered way through a year of teaching is at the heart of The Complete 4. It is my experience that current teaching in reading and writing tends to focus on genre, with not enough attention to process, strategies, and conventions. Experience with all four components is essential for our children to thrive as readers and writers.

"My goodness," you may be thinking at this point, "that sounds great in theory, and I agree that our children need those skills to be powerful readers and writers, but how would I go about putting such a system in place in my classroom? It seems it could be a bit complicated, and the last thing I want is to confuse myself and my students with my teaching."

Please rest assured that I am very aware of your feelings. I have found in my work with teachers that they start off excited by the ideas behind The Complete 4, then become concerned that implementing the components in their classroom will require overhauling their teaching practice, which would be either too challenging or too cumbersome to undertake. They finally reach an understanding that The Complete 4 framework is not only doable in their classroom, and respectful of them as teachers, it also *simplifies their teaching and gives them more time for more effective teaching of reading and writing.*

Yes, teaching with The Complete 4 components, which emphasize being a skilled reader and writer, will ultimately provide more time for you in the classroom. The Complete 4 is an analytical framework within which to plan and integrate your teaching. It is a guide for designing a year of reading and writing instruction that is comprehensive, effective, logical, fun, and incorporates whatever personal elements of teaching reading and writing that are crucial for you. It is not a dogmatic program; it is a flexible framework or guide into which you can powerfully fit your own teaching. The Complete 4 answers the critical questions: WHAT do I teach, WHY do I teach it, WHEN do I teach it, and HOW do I teach it?

For many years we have had a lot of people telling us, sometimes dictating to us, HOW to teach, insisting that we implement all kinds of structures that are supposedly certain to improve our reading and writing instruction. Such structures and programs are superimposed on our teaching, running roughshod over what we know works with our students. Let me be crystal clear that The Complete 4 is designed to honor and integrate your personal teaching style and beliefs, for who better than you knows the students you are working with and what will best enable them to become excellent readers and writers? What The Complete 4 does is to provide the framework for designing and planning your teaching so that it will be maximally effective over the course of the year.

If we always keep in mind that our goal is to educate our students to become the best readers and writers they can be, The Complete 4 flows inevitably and logically forward. WHAT will we teach to ensure that we give our students the skills and abilities they need to reach that goal? WHY are we teaching in the way we are—will the teaching we are engaged in promote our goal? WHEN are we teaching these skills—does our teaching make sense in an orderly fashion over time? And finally, HOW are we teaching—are we teaching to both the whole group and to our individual students in practical, sensible ways?

The Complete 4 is a system for building a truly balanced year of powerful reading and writing instruction through the implementation of flexible, integrated units of study, a system that has grown out of my response to the four questions above.

Understanding a Unit of Study Within The Complete 4

The components of The Complete 4 are as follows:

Process	Genre	Strategy	Conventions

I use these four components to plan my year's units of study. I define units of study as specific time-bound cycles of deliberately connected lessons. There are stages to each unit, which I will describe for you in Chapter 5. For now, it is important to note that I plan my units at each grade level using The Complete 4 system to guide me. If I know that I have good balance among these Complete 4 components, I am much more confident in my teaching, knowing that my students are getting a healthy menu of lessons, literature, and modeling.

I would like for you to be able to name the teaching you already do as units of study. You will see in the accompanying chart that all the units I list for you should feel very realistic in your teaching and very doable for you. Remember, The Complete 4 system is meant to simplify your teaching life. Let's look at a chart outlining The Complete 4 in more detail as it relates directly to our teaching practice in the classroom.

You can see in the chart on page 23 that there are many choices of units within each Complete 4 component category. A key to organizing your teaching is to be aware of the units you are teaching and will teach throughout the year, to be conscious of how to incorporate elements of your teaching practice into the units, and to create curriculum through the units.

The Complete 4™ Units of Study in the Teaching of Reading and Writing

Reading and writing are subject areas that require a curriculum. Teaching inside units of study helps you to organize your thinking and maximize your teaching time. The Complete 4 may be utilized to help you develop major and minor strands in your units. Use LitLife's standards-rich, practical categories to help plan your timetable across a year of teaching.

Process 30 percent	Genre 30 percent	Strategy 20 percent	Conventions 20 percent
• Creating a reading/ writing community (ARCH) • Reading/writing identity • Stamina • Pacing • Fluency • Conferring • Peer conferring • Partnerships • Text clubs • Text talk • Book choice • Making plans and setting goals • Storytelling • Independence • Mentors • Tools of a reader/writer • Content area reading/writing • Writing about reading • Assessment and reflection • Revision • Writing under timed conditions • Finding writing ideas • Developing writing ideas • The Four Prompts (Observe, Wonder, Remember, Imagine) • Techno-literacy	**Narrative:** • Fiction • Memoir • Personal essay • Short story • Play • Folktales • Mysteries • Historical fiction • Fantasy • Science fiction • Series • Biography **Persuasive Nonfiction:** • Persuasive essay • Book blurbs/reviews • Literary essay/criticism • Editorial • Debate • Speech • Feature Article **Informational Nonfiction:** • News article • Essay • Biography • All-about book • How-to text • Question/answer book **Poetry** **Letters** **Picture books** **Standardized tests**	• Monitoring for meaning • Rereading • Activating schema • Making connections • Visualizing • Determining importance • Inferring • Prereading (predictions, book walk, cover, blurb) • Interpretation • Critical analysis • Character analysis • Story elements • Retelling • Summarizing • Note-taking • Research • Theme study • Author study • Organizational structures • Revision • Writing to a prompt • Studying craft strategies • Close study of an anchor text • Reading like a writer	• Concepts of print • Word attack/word-solving skills • Grammar • End punctuation • Pausing punctuation • Linking punctuation • Dialogue • Capitalization • Fluency and phrasing • Syntax (sentence structure) • Sentence types/variety • Parts of speech • Editing • Spelling strategies and resources • Conventions as a craft tool • Paragraphs • Roots, prefixes, suffixes • Word origins

© LitLife 2003-2007

Let me lead you through a practical example of exactly what I mean when I speak of The Complete 4 as an integrated framework to maximize the effectiveness of what you are already undoubtedly doing in the classroom.

Complete 4 Instruction: Focused and Flexible

During your teaching time with students, you will engage in periods of direct instruction, during which you will want to teach them something explicit they can use in their reading and writing. These wonderful moments occur through-out the day, sometimes at the most unexpected times, but we can be certain that over the long haul they regularly occur when we are teaching to our students as a class. I call this time period Focused Instruction (FI).

Focused Instruction

Whether your kids gather together on a rug for their Focused Instruction in reading and writing, or whether they sit at their desks, this is the time when you are addressing the entire class together as a learning community.

At this highly personal level of teaching practice, The Complete 4 defers to and respects your choice for how best to engage your students in this learning. There are no requirements in The Complete 4 as to how you specifically teach in the classroom. My experience repeatedly has reinforced my belief that teachers are professionals, and they do not like it at all when people tell them how they should be teaching in their classrooms. What The Complete 4 does instead is to provide a structure for your teaching to reach its highest potential.

Think of the teaching of reading and writing under The Complete 4 as being the (1) planned and thoughtful (2) use of instructional tools and techniques (3) a teacher is comfortable using in her classroom (4) to teach discrete skills to students (5) through predesigned units of study (6) which at the end of the year provide students with exposure to the full range of skills they need at their grade level to be proficient readers and writers.

What It Looks Like With a Read-Aloud

Let me show you an example of how this works in practice, using one of my favorite instructional tools, the read-aloud.

1. **Planned and thoughtful teaching.** Going into each period of Focused Instruction with your students, you should know what you will be teaching, why you are teaching it, and how you will be teaching it. This clarity reflects good overall planning of your yearlong teaching, which in turn makes your teaching point inherently useful to your students and likely to be absorbed by them, since it will fall naturally into a progression of learning they have engaged in since the beginning of the year. Let's say, for example, that you are in the middle of a narrative unit, and you have planned to use this Focused Instruction time to integrate a teaching moment on punctuation (dialogue marks).

2. **Use of instructional tools and techniques.** In this case, your technique will be the read-aloud, and your tool will be the text you are reading from. Which text and how you choose to do your read-aloud are entirely up to you.

3. **A teacher is comfortable using in her classroom.** If you have a class-room library with a great assortment of books, a rug for the students to gather on, and a chair nearby for you to sit in, this works perfectly. But if you prefer to teach this lesson with the kids sitting at their desks, using text from a basal reader or other structured reading text, that is an equally and completely valid way to present the Focused Instruction. Your choice of text and how to present it are wholly dependent on the particular circumstances you are in—your experience level, the type and quantity of resources available to you, your knowledge of your students and what environment best enables them to learn, and the type of teaching style that works best for you and makes you most effective.

4. **To teach discrete skills to students.** During this Focused Instruction time period, your main goal is to teach students how to use dialogue marks to make writing powerful, to model how the author of the text you are reading aloud uses dialogue marks, and to give students a task to do after the read-aloud to try this new learning in their own writing.

5. **Through predesigned units of study.** The unit of study provides the framework for the teaching. Your Focused Instruction on dialogue marks is one piece of a jigsaw puzzle—small in comparison to a year's worth of teaching about writing and reading, but absolutely critical for the complete picture.

6. **Which at the end of the year provide students with exposure to the full range of skills they need at their grade level to be proficient readers and writers.** Just as a read-aloud focusing on dialogue marks and their use and impact is one part of a bigger unit of study, each unit of study is one part of a complete learning plan for the course of an entire year. The year should be designed so that it flows in an integrated and cohesive way from beginning to end, with all skills having been taught by the end of the year in a logical way so that they build upon each other throughout the year.

Finally, just as units of study should flow logically through the year, there should be coherency across grade levels in each school so that the teaching we impart to our students should flow logically through all the years they are with us in our school.

Like the beautiful Russian nesting dolls, each opening to reveal another doll in its core, Complete 4 teaching evolves in a natural yet systematic way throughout the year. There is a teaching point within Focused Instruction within a day of teaching within a unit within a year within a continuum through the years.

The Research That Undergirds
The Complete 4

The Complete 4 is based on the understanding that four components are integral to reading and writing instruction: process, genre, strategy, and conventions. The Complete 4 system itself is unique in that it LINKS all four of these components in such a way that you can build calendars, design instruction, and plan assessments from it.

An extensive body of research has shown us how important each of these components is in creating a theoretically sound instructional approach that supports the most effective readers and writers. But until now, there has not been a system that integrates all these parts. The Complete 4 is that system.

LitLife

I am the executive director of LitLife, a national organization providing on-site professional development for teachers in the areas of reading and writing instruction. My colleagues and I do our fieldwork in classrooms and refine our ideas using feedback we get from you, the ultimate experts. Our learning has come from many hours spent alongside students in your classrooms, revising and expanding our ideas on the basis of what we find truly works: kids are reading and writing more frequently, in the ways I describe in this book. Teacher satisfaction in our client schools is soaring because teachers are feeling both excited and comfortable with the process and with the outcomes of The Complete 4 system. Best of all, students demonstrate their satisfaction through their eagerness to read and write inside this complete framework. They relish the whole-class journeys, as well as the attention to their individual growth.

Four Components

Here is what the wide body of research is saying to us about the key components of The Complete 4:

Process

Great teachers such as Don Murray (2003), Don Graves (2005), and Lucy Calkins (1994) have taught us that process is as critical to human development in literacy as the products themselves, and that students who think reflectively about their work are stronger readers and writers because of it. Mary Ellen Giacobbe (2007) addresses time and response as essential to a child's growth in literacy, as does Nancie Atwell (2004) talking about older students in the same kinds of powerful ways. Other process elements such as fluency have become widely recognized as key to the learning process in both reading and writing (Opitz, 2007; Rasinski 2003; Leograndis, 2006). In 2002, the National Reading Panel made strong connections between fluency and comprehension (National Institute of Child Health and Human Development 2002). Fluency, while not an end in itself, contributes to overall success in reading and writing.

Genre

Heather Lattimer (2003), Georgia Heard (1989), and many other important voices in the field have discussed the value of genre as a lens through which children come to understand forms of writing and reading in the world. Irene Fountas and Gay Su Pinnell (2006) note that written language performs multiple functions and assumes a wide array of forms or genres. Students become powerful readers and writers as they learn to comprehend and control various genres, understanding how to shift their linguistic style and shape their evolving text depending on the purpose for which they are writing and reading. For example, students draw from different syntactic structures and vocabulary and assume different pragmatic stances when they craft a poem, pen a persuasive essay, or jot down notes about a homework assignment for an absent friend.

Strategy

Debbie Miller (2002), Ellin Keene and Susan Zimmerman (2007), P. David Pearson (2002), Michael Pressley (2005), and other prominent language researchers and educators have documented that effective readers use active comprehension strategies while reading. They make inferences, ask questions, forge connections, determine ideas, and synthesize what they read. A wide range of strategic actions work in concert to support expansive thinking. Carl Anderson (2000), Katie Wood Ray (1999), and Lucy Calkins (1994) have demonstrated that even the youngest writers can think metacognitively and planfully about their writing.

Conventions

Diane Snowball and Faye Bolton in *Teaching Spelling K–8* (1999), Sandra Wilde in *Spelling Strategies and Patterns* (2007), and Constance Weaver in *Teaching Grammar in Context* (1996) address the issue of how to teach the mechanics—grammar, spelling, and punctuation—in meaningful ways. Jeff Anderson in *Mechanically Inclined* (2005) makes the work of conventions relevant and meaningful to students by bringing its uses and purposes to the fore, and teaching conventions and grammar in active, purposeful ways.

Focused Instruction

I will speak often throughout this book about the balance in your teaching and planning between focused whole-class instruction and the opportunities our students have for Independent Practice, which is integrally connected to this Focused Instruction.

Dick Allington (2002) notes that in typical classrooms it is not unusual to find that children read and write for as little as ten percent of the day. Kelly Gallagher also reports in *Deeper Reading* (2004) that students in the upper grades are reading for no more than seven minutes a day! And yet our common sense tells us what we must do to get better at the thing we want to do well. In *Understanding Reading* (2004), Frank Smith demonstrates that the complex human act of reading with its orchestration of linguistic, physiological, psychological, and social systems is necessarily learned through the act of reading itself.

Jeni Pollack Day et al. (2002) note three characteristics of a balanced (what I call comprehensive) approach to reading instruction (and The Complete 4 extends this to writing), which should be foundational. The approach is:

- Built on research
- Views teachers as informed decision makers and is therefore flexible
- Built on a comprehensive view of literacy

The Complete 4 is a system that is built on research, views you as informed decision makers, and is, therefore, deeply flexible. What's more, it draws from a comprehensive view of literacy and regards students as active meaning makers, who act on their world to learn about it (Wells & Hart-Hewins, 1999). The Complete 4 system shows you how to integrate the components that will enable you to address the wide spectrum of written language and teach to your fullest potential so you can help your students reach theirs.

What If You Use a Basal?

As you can tell from my description of a read-aloud in The Complete 4, if you use a basal reader, or what is now sometimes called an organized reading program, you still can and should plan your year according to The Complete 4 units. Many basal readers are organized according to thematic units. While these units have no correlation to a continuum across grades, what is nice about the basals is that they contain thoughtfully chosen texts that can be very useful to you as you implement your Complete 4 units of study.

And whether you use a basal or not, The Complete 4 model requires that Focused Instruction includes time for a read-aloud or a shared-reading opportunity. The texts for this shared reading can come from your basal collection and can be used for whole-class instruction when studying author's craft, for example. Purchase overhead sheets for students to place over their basal pages to write on, marking places where they love the language or have a question about the text. The basals become a mini-workbench your students can use for a quick practice lesson when you meet on the rug for Focused Instruction.

The basal excerpts can be used effectively for small-group instruction during Independent Practice. For example, if you observe that four of your students are having trouble inferring from text, you can use one of the basal readings for this small group as their short shared guided text, which means that you'll have multiple copies readily available. I would not recommend that you use the basal during your students' independent reading, as your students should each be reading texts at their appropriate reading levels. Differentiating texts for independent reading is an enormously valuable and effective teaching practice for helping children become better readers.

The basal texts can be used effectively during the Wrap-Up, however, in that you can reinforce your main point of the day through the texts in the collection. Make them work for you. Try to be comfortable mixing and matching them to your Complete 4 units. The basals' themes are generally about community, nature, friendship, or animals. If you are doing a theme study, you could select one of the basal themes and show your students how the texts are grouped together. But for most Complete 4 units, you can use any of the basal text excerpts to suit your needs.

You can use the basal text to support your process studies. For example, if you are doing a unit on reading-identity building, you could have your students browse through all the varieties of texts in the basal collection, finding the ones that really resonate with them as readers. For a conventions unit, you could have the students work in partnerships looking at basal excerpts to find examples of elegant sentences or well-constructed paragraphs. The point is that The Complete 4 works equally well, whether or not you are using basals in your classroom.

Does The Complete 4 Meet the Needs of All Students?

The Complete 4 works with all students, and it works with the materials available in all classrooms. The Complete 4 is a teaching framework whose specific implementation can—and should—be varied to adjust to the specific needs and strengths of the particular students you are working with. One of the strengths of The Complete 4 is that it forces thoughtful planning, always keeping your teaching goals at the forefront and meaning that you will always be conscious of the needs of each of your individual students. For instance, English language learners (ELLs) might need more of a focus on conventions work to become familiar more quickly with the quirks and formalities of English. And your choice of text will vary depending on your students. But the basic framework remains completely worthwhile and useful. I am passionate about the need for a complete system that embraces the needs of all students, from the most struggling learners to the most sophisticated. The Complete 4 balances your year and your daily instruction so that students from both ends of this spectrum get what they need and also have the chance to work with texts and skills at their independent levels.

A Note for Teachers of English Language Learners

English language learners are the fastest growing percentage of K–12 students in the United States. As noted by Freeman and Freeman (2007), "The U.S. Census Bureau reports that about one in five students in public schools lives in a home where English is not the primary language. The Bureau reports that by 2030, nearly 40 percent of the school-age population will speak languages other than English at home" (p. 5). The time is now to reassess current practice for ELLs in the literacy environment. Our research in schools shows us that teachers are struggling to find ways to address the multiplicity of perspectives and voices in one room. Data from 52 high-risk schools used to compare the progress of English learners and English-only students on a variety of literacy assessments found that a much higher percentage of Spanish-speaking students remained at the beginning reading level through the primary grades (Helman, 2005).

When I started my work in classrooms of the deaf many years ago, I was fascinated by the idea that a classroom could provide a rich oasis of immersion into language that would include all children. I wanted to give my students every opportunity their hearing peers had to feel the cascading power of the English language and to be empowered by it. I saw my deaf students as the ultimate second-language learners. Their first language was entirely visual, and so the challenges of the phonetics of English were even more profound.

What I found was that the more the child was seen as "language deprived," the more likely that child was to receive intensive remediation that felt outside of and not at all connected to authentic reading experiences. The child then developed a negative view of literacy development, seeing himself to be outside the inner sphere. The work seemed full of tricks, pitfalls, and challenges, a place the child feared to go. It was only when I began to imagine my classroom as a haven, a literacy sanctuary, that I began to construct an environment of authentic reading and writing experiences, scaffolded by whole-group experiences to small-group experiences to Independent Practice, where children were reading and writing at their comfort levels. I used a wide range of literature to "pour" words into our sanctuary, and we began to think about ourselves as readers and writers who were constantly growing and changing as the year unfolded. I found my kids came to love reading and writing in these ways, and, therefore, some of the skill building we also did became far less onerous because they could see how it connected to their own writing and reading.

Later, in my work at P.S. 95 in the Bronx, New York, I taught many students from the Dominican Republic and found the same thing to be true: If students feel compelled, and if they feel included in an authentic literacy experience and the world of words, they are much more likely to strive for an understanding of the architecture of the English language itself.

At LitLife, we are creating curriculum that employs both the structure of Focused Instruction and Independent Practice. The ELL is not on the fringe, not on the outside waiting to learn English before he can participate in the rich content-learning of the classroom. Like all students in the community, the ELL is part of the academic journey. And yet, during the time dedicated to Independent Practice, this same student may be drawing and labeling a picture for a story, whereas an English speaker may be at the writing level. During reading time, the ELL will be reading a text well matched to his level in fluency, decoding, and comprehension, as are the other students. By establishing regular, daily

opportunities for Independent Practice connected to whole-group instruction, the English language learner receives a complete literacy education.

Freeman and Freeman (2007) describe six keys to working successfully with English language learners. The first key is "Know your students." The most effective instruction is "responsive teaching." Frank Smith urges us to respond to what the child is trying to do. When we know our students, understand their cultural backgrounds and experiences, and observe closely the ways in which they are striving to make sense of their new cultural and linguistic experiences, we're able to create learning experiences that fully support and accelerate their own drive to learn.

The second key is "Teach language through content." The Complete 4 enables students to use reading and writing to learn about the world—students aren't restricted to learning only the structure of language. As with all students, the English language learner needs both instruction and opportunities to practice in *all* The Complete 4 categories, the route to becoming an effective reader and writer. In keeping with solid theories of second-language acquisition (Krashen, 2003), The Complete 4 shows teachers how to teach both language and content at the same time. Indeed, the conventions component of The Complete 4 is designed to connect the work of grammar, punctuation, and word work to the authentic reading and writing lives of students. In this way we can meet the challenge Fillmore and Snow (2000) assign to working with ELLs: "To provide the kind of feedback that students need for polishing their writing, teachers need to understand English structure, discuss structured features of written language with their students, and explicitly teach them how to write effectively" (p. 31). Complex, accurate language develops most successfully when students have compelling reasons to use the language to learn about the world.

The third key is "Organize curriculum around themes." ELLs are more fully supported when all lessons relate to a unifying theme with similar language and concepts. Since The Complete 4 is organized around units of study, it lends itself naturally to thematic teaching. Everything—from the lessons to the anchor texts—relates to a particular topic or theme, which infuses the target language (English) with meaning, making it more likely ELLs will receive what Krashen calls "comprehensible input," critical for successful language learning.

The fourth key is to draw on students' primary languages and cultures whenever possible. Even when you don't speak the primary language(s) of your students, find ways to involve family members or other members from your ELLs' communities who can share the child's cultural and linguistic traditions and help bridge the two worlds that ELLs typically face daily.

The fifth key centers on meaningful reading and writing. ELLs may become good decoders of English but fail to construct meaning from English texts. The Complete 4 organizes all literacy instruction around process, genre, strategy, and conventions, and at the heart of all four is meaning. The goal is to use these four essential components to make sense of text across a range of genres while helping students create their own meaningful written texts.

Finally, ELLs, like other students, need academic language to succeed in school. The scaffolding support of The Complete 4 lends itself naturally to instruction that best supports ELLs so they can meet the challenge of reading, writing, and discussing academic content. As García and Beltrán (2003) remind us, "English language learners must be given ample opportunities to employ the English language, and cooperative activities are particularly conducive to promoting the use of the language structures targeted for instruction, practice and application" (p. 217).

The Complete 4 in conjunction with the six keys of successful work with ELLs assures that we can avoid reducing language to a "single skill or a single domain, absent of any social context or link to human experience" (Del Vecchio & Guerrero, 1995, p. 83). In The Complete 4 classroom, all language and literacy learning is folded into the vital work of learning about the world, and in this way, school becomes a rich, vibrant experience for all students.

Closing Thoughts

The Complete 4 is an extraordinarily powerful framework for the teaching of reading and writing. It works with all types of teachers, in all types of classrooms, with all types of students. It is analytical, thoughtful, and goal oriented. It honors the professionalism of teachers and respects their experience and knowledge of their communities and students. It supports teachers without dictating to them. It makes the teaching of reading and writing more natural and effective. And The Complete 4 does all this while giving teachers the wonderful feeling that, regardless of what the clock says, they now have more time for the teaching of reading and writing.

Let's look at The Complete 4 more closely.

CHAPTER 2

The Complete 4 Components Up Close and Personal

It is my heartfelt hope that you will embrace The Complete 4 as you would an old friend you have not seen for a while; the ideas you see will likely be familiar. You know that these are the tenets of your natural teaching. What I am doing by inviting you into The Complete 4 experience is helping you simplify and structure your natural teaching instincts and practices. The framework does not override your natural instincts; it gives them a structure so that your intuitive teaching can be even more powerful.

To get the full sense of what I mean by The Complete 4 components, let's take a quick journey through each of the four.

Process: Alluring Intangibles

Whenever I talk to teachers about what they most want for their students as readers and writers, their lists are full of intangibles. We want our students to love to read and write; we want them to become lifelong readers and writers; we want them to think and talk deeply about books. And yet, our curriculum is full of tangibles—cold, heartless tangibles. Tangibles are easier to plan for and easier to name. And given the emphasis on standards and testing, we expect the stacks of mandated tests our kids are taking will be assessing those tangibles.

Interestingly, though, even our state standards and state reading and writing tests reflect the desire to assess in some way the habits of mind of effective readers and writers. And I consider this to be the perfect example of where state assessments are actually guiding us toward better teaching. Let's give "teach to the test" a new meaning. No longer will it signify cramming for a state-mandated examination by running rote drills and repetitive worksheets. Instead, let's accept that the exams are looking for an understanding of and facility with things like process, a skill set critical to any reader and writer, and let's embrace how lucky we are that the people in charge of designing the test see things this way, and teach the best process units we can to our children. We will simultaneously interest them, give them essential skills they need to become good readers and writers, *and* prepare them for the test. Let us bring intangibles like process back to our curriculum, and back to front and center stage in our classrooms.

The Complete 4 model not only reestablishes process studies as paramount in our teaching, but reinvents them, too. My intention is to provide you with concrete, doable, outcome-based, accessible units in process, just like the kind of teaching we do in the more tangible subject areas.

Understanding a Process Unit

Process units may be categorized under the four headings of Identities, Capacities, Collaborations, and Student/teacher roles.

- **Identities**
  Identity units are clustered sets of lessons that address, in an explicit manner, the kinds of behaviors we want our children to demonstrate as readers and writers, which reflect who they are and who they are becoming as readers and writers.

- **Capacities**
  Capacities units are those that explicitly address clusters of

lessons relating to the muscles we want our kids to develop as readers and writers, particularly stamina, fluency, and independence.

- **Collaborations**

  Collaborations units explicitly address clusters of lessons relating to the ways children interact with one another through their own reading and writing experiences. These include partnerships, clubs, and other informal conversations. Clusters of lessons on the roles of students and teachers explicitly address the techniques and steps that children go through to work with one another in reading and writing.

- **Student/teacher roles**

  Units on student/teacher roles explore expectations and behaviors both teachers and students must manifest for the reading and writing times to go smoothly and productively. These include units on conferring and classroom routines, as well as explicit instruction on how to use the tools of readers and writers.

Process units range from one week to four weeks long. They spiral up through time, just as any other unit of study would. For example, if you are doing a process study on conferring in kindergarten, your lessons might be mainly about what students could be doing in their Independent Practice while you are conferring with individual students. This could be a three-day unit. In fifth grade, your focus on conferring as the subject of a process study might illuminate the conversational moves between teacher and student that create an effective conference. Another process unit might help students plan the agenda for a serious conversation they will have with their teacher about setting goals for the coming weeks in reading and writing.

These process units ensure that students have the tools they need to delve into all other areas of learning to read and write—from nuts and bolts practicalities, such as where to actually go in the room during certain lessons and where to store materials they will need for their reading and writing, to much more sophisticated interactions and instruction in the upper grades as to the nature of conversation between teacher and student, and the best modes of communicating when working in groups or with partners. Let's take a closer look at each one.

Identities

The essential unit of study on process is the concept of identity. We need to study with our kids the processes of building a sense of oneself as a reader and writer, creating a community of readers and writers, finding reading/writing role models, and reflecting and setting goals as a reader and writer. Any child who does not see himself as a reader/writer, or as capable of becoming a good reader/writer, will never become one.

To help you begin to understand how this kind of process unit takes shape in the classroom, take a look at this chart:

Name of Process Unit	K–2 Process Unit	3–5 Process Unit
Building a sense of oneself as a reader/writer (Identity)	**Habits of a reader/writer:** • carrying books around • carrying writing tools around • reading the world (signs, environmental print) • celebrating small steps (first picture walks, telling stories through pictures, oral storytelling) • using the reader/writer toolbox—spelling strategies and word attack strategies • understanding where, when, and with whom you like to read and write	**Habits of a reader/writer:** • carrying books around • carrying writing tools around • using the reader/writer toolbox—strategies for addressing difficult vocabulary • reading from a wide range of genres and writing in a wide range of genres • understanding influences on self as a reader/writer • growing sense of pride in length of time and number of texts read and pages written • understanding where, when, and with whom you like to read and write

This chart outlines one critical process unit of study focusing on identity: building a sense of oneself as a reader and a writer. You will notice that for the purposes of this book I have broken down the units into K–2 and 3–5 grade divisions. Of course, each grade level could have its particular components, and each school will have its own particular components. I present these, though, in keeping with my goal of giving you a flexible framework. What I have set forth in the charts throughout the book is what works best on a general basis— but I urge you to customize these charts to fit the specifics of the teaching environment in which you find yourself. If the chart works for you, use it as is; if it needs modifying, tweak it so that it is just right for you.

You will notice that some components are the same at both the K–2 level and the 3–5 level. I want to make it very clear that when a component of a unit of study is repeated across grade levels, it is not intended to be taught in the same way at the different grade levels. It is my belief that it is fundamentally boring and inappropriate to teach children the same unit at different grade levels. Which is not to say that some components of process units should not be repeated every single year—they should be, but in a form appropriate to the children in your classroom.

Your children are building identity all the time. From the moment they enter school, they are unconsciously or consciously asking themselves the questions, Who am I here? How do I fit in? How do I stand out? In the act of reading, a child interacts with text. There is potential for change in that

interaction. Process units on identity address this point of change. The child comes to know him- or herself: I am becoming the kind of reader who reads nonfiction; I am becoming the kind of reader who reads chapter books; I am the kind of reader who allows myself to be moved by strong feeling in text; I am the kind of reader who knows what to do when I come to a word I don't know.

In the act of writing, the student interacts with ideas, his or her own. And those ideas become text. The child continues now to interact with this new text, the text of his or her creation. An identity unit in writing addresses that powerful issue of oneself in relation to one's own ideas and one's own text. The child begins to ask questions that lead to deeper thinking, more writing on the page, and further growth. These questions include the following: What kind of writing do I most like to do? What gets in my way as a writer? What inspires me? How do I tackle difficult spelling? The child formulates ideas about him- or herself. Again, the identity is being shaped by your gentle facilitation. The child says, "I am the kind of writer who uses the poetry of Robert Frost to nourish my own writing"; "I am the kind of writer who writes most fluently when I am writing fiction"; "I am the kind of writer who formulates ideas on note cards and then creates an essay out of them"; "I am the kind of writer who likes to write plays and poems with a partner"; "I am the kind of writer who uses my sticky notes in the block area to tell stories about my creations."

Capacities

A second critical area of process units is what I call "capacities." During these units, children should be given more choice regarding what they are reading and what they are writing, so your lessons can focus on their capacities for strength in the areas of reading and writing. In a fluency unit, for example, your lessons are all about what will help your kids become "smooth" readers and writers. For Danny, fiction writing helps him write fast and long and strong. For Sarah, writing sets of editorials is what gets her to that fast, long, and strong point. Your lessons in both reading and writing will focus on what fluency is, demonstrating through your own example and also using student models and samples. Units include stamina, fluency, independence, reading/writing in the content areas, reading/writing on the Internet, reading/writing for standardized tests, writing about reading, writing under timed conditions, and writing in response to a prompt.

Here is an example of a capacities process unit of study on independence, again broken into K–2 and 3–5 categories:

Name of Process Unit	K–2 Process Unit	3–5 Process Unit
Independence (Capacities)	• Students will use materials such as writing paper, pencils and sticky notes, book baskets. • Students will move about the room purposefully. • Students will participate in informal partner talk. • Students will turn pages of books to tell a story (picture walks). • Students will begin to stretch sounds of words. • Students will select books for reading, and topic choice for writing ideas.	• Students will make book choices. • Students will develop writing ideas. • Students will use resources, including dictionaries, Internet, and grammar references. • Students will move from one book to the next. • Students will begin a new text. • Students will begin a new writing piece. • Students will prepare for a reading or writing conference.

You can see again that, as with all process studies, the skills learned are enormously beneficial to learning to read and write, but they are also very useful skills for functioning effectively as a student in all aspects of classroom life. The independence achieved by learning how to prepare for a successful reading or writing conference translates very well into planning in all content areas. Learning how to speak informally to partners about the subject being studied raises not only the level of classroom discussion and understanding in the content areas, but leads to better communication skills in general in the social life of the classroom. As you do process units of study in your classroom, you will repeatedly be struck by their value not just to literacy teaching, but to the general tone and overall quality of interactions in your classroom.

Techno-literacy is a new entry to our process category. Students are reading and writing in ways you and I might never have imagined possible a mere ten years ago. Technology has inspired us to imagine new ways to talk with our students about reading and writing strategies. The Internet requires a faster eye, a keen sense of distilling information down to its key words, and massive internal editing to lead us to the nuggets of communication we pass back and forth among friends and colleagues known as e-mail. Never before in the history of civilization has such extensive access to written forms of literacy been available, and never before has there been such an opportunity to reach so many people with our own writing. It is a double-edged sword, however, for what allows the incredible access and distribution is the lack of filters. So while we are in a golden era of communication, one of our main jobs in working with our students on process in these times is to teach them how to filter and assess the worth of all the written material available to them online.

Here is an illumination of the aspects of a unit in techno-literacy and the spiraling up through the grade levels:

Name of Process Unit	K–2 Process Unit	3–5 Process Unit
Techno-literacy (Capacities)	• Students will practice writing simple e-mails to friends in their class. • Students will use search engines to research favorite animals. • Students will talk with their teacher about how to know what is true and what is not true on the Internet by discussing simple Internet texts. • Students will practice using Internet reading strategies to build stamina and learn how to skim across an Internet Web page.	• Students will learn how to craft a series of related e-mail communications with a partner, continuing a train of thought and building off the other person's ideas. • Students will conduct research using Internet search engines and at least three Web sites of value to support their ideas and collect evidence to bolster an argument. • Students will continue to explore the question of how we authenticate veracity using Internet sources. • Students will reflect on the metacognitive strategies used when reading a Web site.

You can see that the focus is on the actual physical mechanics of creating a communication (writing an e-mail to a friend), along with a reflective component, such as how to determine the veracity and value of a Web site, and what our thinking is as we engage as readers of Web text to make those determinations.

Collaborations

One particularly powerful way to engage children in reading and writing is to have them work with and interact with their classmates. To do so productively in a fun way that really benefits their burgeoning reading and writing skills, students need to understand how to talk with and interact with one another when discussing their reading and writing. Interacting and working with other students is, as you have just seen, part of the capacities unit as well. Let me take a moment here to point out that such mixing and border crossing is entirely correct. The Complete 4 is designed as a completely flexible tool. When you discover something that works in your teaching, please do not worry that it may not be the appropriate time to use it because it is not part of the unit currently at hand. Use your judgment and professional sense as a good teacher—when a teaching moment arrives, take it. Bend borders, put topics in two categories, mix and match as needed to teach your students. The flexibility of The Complete 4 in practice is its most basic strength.

I would urge a strong focus on collaborations, as the peripheral benefits to everyday life in your classroom are abundant. In addition to helping every student learn, the collaborations allow every student to get to know every other student in the classroom as a learner, and as a learner to be respected and appreciated.

Units on collaboration involve students working and talking together, and include partnerships, text talks, text clubs, and writing clubs.

Here is a sample unit on collaborations, focusing on partnerships:

Name of Process Unit	K–2 Process Unit	3–5 Process Unit
Partnerships (Collaborations)	• Students will set up physical space for partners to talk efficiently and comfortably. • Students will share materials (book baskets, one shared text, writing materials). • Students will talk with partners (making text connections, retelling, asking questions).	• Students will set up physical space for partners to talk efficiently and comfortably. • Students will share materials (book baskets, one shared text, writing materials). • Students will talk productively with a partner (making text connections, retelling, asking questions, seeing text-to-text connections, conducting theme-based conversations). • Students will read and write outcome-based projects. • Students will talk reflectively about the successes and challenges of the conversation. • Students will sustain a thread of a conversation across two or more days ("durable talk").

You can see that the skills taught here are both active and reflective—from the actual mechanics of how and where to sit when conversing with your partner, to techniques for talking in a reflective manner about the conversation you had with your partner.

Student/Teacher Roles

Many process units are really laying the groundwork for effective teaching of reading and writing. Units concerning the roles teacher and students play in different aspects of studying reading and writing give students the understanding of what the meetings and conversations are designed to achieve and how particular styles of interacting will best move toward that outcome. Units on student/teacher roles include what each is expected to do during focused/whole-group instruction, guided/Independent Practice, and conferences.

Here is a sample process unit on student/teacher roles:

Name of Process Unit	K–2 Process Unit	3–5 Process Unit
Student/teacher roles during Focused Instruction (Student/teacher roles)	• Teacher will record thinking on anchor charts. • Students will participate in helping to create anchor charts. • Students will turn and talk to each other and briefly practice a suggested prompt given by the teacher. • Students will use a sticky note and a pen to record brief thinking; students will affirm with a partner or with a teacher what they will do during the Independent Practice.	• Students will develop ideas for the anchor charts in their own notebooks or journals. • Students will come to the mini-lesson with a sample of their own work from the prior day's lesson, prepared to use it as part of the teaching. • Teacher will offer a prompted exercise, at which point students will turn and talk to a partner or may write and record in their notebook/journal; before leaving the common area, students will affirm their plans for the day's or the week's Independent Practice by recording their thinking and their plans in their notebook/journal.

Again, the unit's immediate focus on student/teacher interactions during literacy teaching is paramount, but the benefits to the type and content of their interactions in other areas of study are apparent. This kind of instruction is like money in the bank. When you do this type of work with your students, subsequent units go far more smoothly because you have worked hard to set all the structures in place. Some structures, such as conferring, take some time to establish and require strong Focused Instruction to help their meaning and purpose come clear to your students. As students learn to be more active during Focused Instruction, it has been shown that they are more likely to retain the information you share with them. But these behaviors are not necessarily second nature to your students. Unit opportunities for modeling will help the flow of your classroom management immensely.

Genre: Containers for Thought

For a long time now, genre has been the major focus of teachers in designing and implementing units of study. Teachers have often been asked (or, unfortunately, told) to teach reading and writing through the year in a sequence of genre-based units of study, often of fixed duration and specific sequence. The unworkability of such a system, both theoretically (top heavy in genre and inadequate in other areas) and practically (lack of coordination with other teaching, either in content or timing), has made many teachers loathe working in such a structure.

The Complete 4, with its aversion to such rigidity in both content and practice, and its emphasis on incorporating other aspects of literacy that are critical to the success of our work with kids in the classroom, nonetheless keeps genre as a key focus of units of study throughout the year. However—and this should by now become almost a mantra for you in your teaching and planning—genre units of study should be flexible in design and implementation.

Good readers and writers are well aware that the world is full of genre, and they approach their reading and writing equipped with knowledge about the characteristics and demands of a variety of genre. While basic reading and writing strategies can be applied across genres, there is a particular way an active reader or writer will interact with a specific genre. For example, although white space is a signifier in any genre, from magazine reading to the end of a chapter in a chapter book, white space takes on urgent significance in a poem. It is a deliberate choice by the poet to move us with the silence between words.

A test is its own genre. Students who practice for tests become expert at knowing how to predict in advance what sort of questions will be on the test and gain a familiarity and comfort level with the kind of directions printed at the bottom of every page.

After my daughter took an eighth-grade standardized language arts exam, she said, "It went really well. Every time I have to write a question for a big test, I generally write about Amelia Earhart because I did a research report about her in third grade. Whatever the essay question is on a test, I know it will fit." My daughter knows she can use information she has and mold it to fit the kind of writing she needs to do—she has learned how to take information and present it to the world in a variety of genres. Whether the question is about someone she admires, someone who changed history, someone who changed her perspective on feminism, or a metaphor about flight, the key for my daughter is understanding what she needs to do to fit that knowledge into the right container.

Genres are containers for thought. Hemingway once said that writers write about just two or three ideas their whole lives. The children's book writer Charlotte Zolotow explored themes of loneliness and friendship, and the connections between parents and children, in poetry, picture books, and even a chapter book. We seek different types of genres to satisfy different kinds of needs we have at different times. After 9/11, someone asked the poet laureate Billy Collins why there was so much poetry circulating on the Internet. He said it was because poetry tells the history of the human heart. In the beautiful picture book by Naomi Nye, *Sitti's Secrets*, a Palestinian child writes a letter to convey her big ideas about peace to a wider audience.

When we want to learn how to do something, we seek the genre of a how-to book. The containers serve a function. A recipe is a how-to structure. We come to know it well, and it works for us. Effective readers, as they grow, seek genre depending on their needs at that particular moment, and they also enter into these texts from a variety of stances, knowing and anticipating the structures of genre. For example, when I read a poem, I get ready for the impact of white space on my thinking. When I read a persuasive essay, I want to make sure I know who the author is, what his or her political perspective is, and what the slant of the factual presentation is before I automatically agree or disagree.

One way to illuminate the distinctions among genres and their purposes is to have students practice what I call the genre switch. Give them a prompted topic, such as how to make a friend. Then ask them to write it first as a how-to, second as a persuasive essay, and third as a poem. Emotionally and intellectually, their brains and hearts switch automatically to accommodate the new genre. This experience is a powerful tool that enables our students to understand the powerful and subtle differences in genre.

Understanding a Genre Unit

There are four major categories in genre studies:

- Narrative

- Poetry

- Nonfiction

- Standardized tests

Genre studies are generally from four to six weeks long. Like all units, they spiral up through time. For example, if you are doing a nonfiction study in kindergarten, your focus might be on recognizing the text features of nonfiction—naming what is and what is not nonfiction, recognizing the difference between fiction and nonfiction. In fifth grade, you might focus on thinking critically about who wrote the piece you are reading, and what the author's area of expertise is. Or you may investigate using nonfiction as secondary source material for research.

Genre studies offer wonderful opportunities for tie-ins with content area material. A good selection of varied genre throughout the year can also play a critical role in sustaining a high level of energy and excitement in your classroom. For instance, boys are notorious lovers of nonfiction, and this is a great hook to get them involved in the world of reading and writing.

Though the type of genre will be revisited each year at the different grade levels, great care must be taken not to simply serve up the same unit of study to students. A poetry unit in kindergarten should not simply be repeated with first graders. Instead, working from templates of suggested units of study that are appropriate for first graders, the teacher should use elements of the model unit that are appropriate for her class, modifying them to respond to the particular personalities and learning levels in the room. As always, have a framework, but be flexible in implementing it.

Narrative

When I began teaching at a school for the deaf in Brooklyn, one of my first students was Wayne, a deaf eighth grader from Guyana. He had arrived in this country speaking no English and knowing no sign language. Slowly he began to learn how to sign, along with some English words. During our writing time, Wayne drew many pictures that were not clear to me and the other students in the class, and so it was hard to find out what story he was trying to tell through them. Yet one day, he asked me if he could share one of his pictures with the class. Slowly, slowly he signed, "In Guyana, I was the lonely deaf." Wayne smiled proudly at us. It was the first time we understood that Wayne had been alone as a deaf student at his school. Unlike the others, he had not come from another school for the deaf. The depth of his aloneness struck us so powerfully. This was Wayne's narrative.

Narrative studies are about building a world of story. Hurricane Katrina was something we couldn't really understand or comprehend, though we thought we did—until we heard the story of Henry. Henry had to leave his old dog behind when he was evacuated from the flooding. He left the dog with some food and Henry's favorite sweater, so the dog could have the comfort of those two things in his last hours until the inevitable. In Afghanistan, the meaning of obtaining the simple but most necessary things was made poignantly clear when we read of girls standing in line for 48 hours to register, once they were given the chance to go to school.

Recently I took a group of boys from The Children's Village, a residential school for boys in foster care, to a senior citizens' residence to read together. These two groups could not be more different on the face of it: old, young, separated by years, race, and experience. And we brought them together to sit and share stories.

Walter told Keyon about baseball and playing with his lifelong friends a kind of stickball that had its own Brooklyn rules. Evelyn told Lamar about her life in the Bronx, sitting on her stoop and dreaming her dreams. Albert told Scott about how sad he was that many of the people he loved had died. At the end of our visit, Lamar, age 11, turned to me and whispered, "They are just like us, the people here. Evelyn, she's just like me." The power of narrative brings people together.

There are some structural qualities of narrative that every student should know because not only do they connect us to other people's stories, but they also help us construct communication that enables us to tell our story to others. The qualities are character development, sense of time passing, plot, sense of place/setting, and theme. Narrative encompasses the short story, parts of an essay, a novel, series books, and picture books.

Here is an example of a narrative unit:

Name of Genre Unit	K–2 Genre Unit	3–5 Genre Unit
Narrative	• Students will retell using elements of story. • Students will develop character sketches. • Students will write about a strong sense of place. • Students will read or take picture walks with an attention to story elements. • Students will name elements of story. • Students will use their growing knowledge of story elements to construct their own stories with these elements, both in telling personal stories and in writing fiction based on their own play and storytelling.	• Students will go beyond retelling; instead, they will be able to share the essence of a narrative through conversation about theme and the impact of time on the text. • Students will go beyond identifying story elements and use them to bolster arguments they develop about what they think the big ideas of a text are. • Students will write more extensive narratives using dialogue and character traits as well as change in scene and artful use of time to bolster plot ideas. • Students will write narratives based on their own life experience, and experiment with fictional narratives to explore the use of time and character perspective.

One major occurrence you'll notice as the unit spirals up through the grade levels is, in reading, the shift from identifying story elements to using them in support of arguments, and, in writing, the shift from organic creation of story to a more crafted, structured version. You can also begin to see how opportunities to cross-fertilize your teaching across different elements of The Complete 4 will always be present in your classroom. Teaching your students to write more extensive narratives using dialogue is an excellent opportunity to do a small unit on grammar and conventions regarding the punctuation marks needed for such an exercise.

I call this integrating of different units of study **majoring** and **minoring**—in the example just cited, the major unit of study would be the genre unit of narrative, whereas the minor unit would be a conventions unit on proper punctuation when writing dialogue. See Chapter 4 for more about major and minor units.

Poetry

Michael, one of the boys I work with at The Children's Village, recently said that poetry "makes me feel like I can release everything I have inside real deep." For exactly that reason, poetry is an incredible genre for kids of any age to express their deepest selves.

Over the course of history, poetry has served as a kind of emotional response, like the one Michael talks about, to the state of human affairs. As I mentioned before, there was an outpouring of poetry after 9/11. Anyone who says that poetry is not political is not reading very carefully. Poetry asks us to wake up and pay attention. Poetry provides comfort. Poetry asks a question. Poetry is about the love of language. Poetry addresses emotion, often unabashedly. Poetry has a structure so that when our emotion threatens to get the best of us, poetry provides a container to harness all of that. Poetry is about celebration of the human spirit, of the smallest, tenderest observation. William Carlos Williams wrote a poem about a red wheelbarrow. Years later, we still read this poem as a classic. It reminds you of one thing, and me of another, because it is really about the poet saying, "Stop. Pay attention. Remember."

Czeslaw Milosz wrote a poem about a man in the later part of his life, simply straightening up as he looks out to the distance. Milosz said that the intention of his poetry was as a "revelation of reality" because through intense observation we see that the ordinary is actually miraculous.

I believe a poetry unit has power on so many levels, to inspire through feeling, and to awe through the beauty and delight of a highly structured genre.

Here is an example of a poetry unit:

Name of Genre Unit	K–2 Genre Unit	3–5 Genre Unit
Poetry	• Students will become immersed in the sound of poetic language, including lullabies, chants, and jump rope rhymes. • Students will become aware of poetry elements, including rhyme, white space, repetition, and line breaks. • Students will read and identify some structures of poetry, including the haiku, the couplet, and free verse. • Students will write in the same structures to represent close observations, wonderings, memories, and uses of the imagination.	• Students will make use of reading and writing strategies to read poetry actively, visualizing images as they read, making connections to other poems and poets, and uncovering metaphor from the concrete ideas presented by the poet. • Students will become familiar with a wider range of structures including the sonnet, the cinquain, and more complex free verse; they will write inside these structures; they will deepen their understanding of poetry from around the world; they will write and read free verse using both humor and seriousness to convey ideas. • Students will continue to deepen their knowledge of craft, using repetition to connect to their themes, using white space to signify silence to their readers, and using line breaks to convey meaning.

Poetry is an especially wonderful unit of study for younger kids because so much of poetry has to do with sound and rhythm, which children can understand and really get a feel for at a very young age. As with our other units in The Complete 4, as we move through the grade levels, craft considerations (both noticing another author's craft and employing elements of craft in one's own poetry) become more important as the children move up through the grades, but they are not ignored in the earlier grades: we identify craft elements, notice them, and celebrate them.

Nonfiction

So much of what we read as adults is nonfiction, so it is important that we expose our students to plentiful nonfiction during the school day. We must make sure that we offer nonfiction in our classroom libraries to the extent that we offer fiction, and that we read aloud from nonfiction as much as we read from fictional texts.

Ensuring the availability and use of nonfiction texts in our classrooms is critically important for another reason. Studies have repeatedly shown that boys tend to gravitate earlier to nonfiction texts as emergent readers. They continue this attachment well beyond the emergent reading stage; in fact, it could easily be argued that many adult men have a pronounced preference for nonfiction. It is a genre that not only provides pleasure and interest to students, but is one that is critically important when looking at reading proficiently—both as a wonderful thing in its own right and also as an absolute necessity for functioning in the world. The ability to read instruction manuals, court summonses, tax notices and forms, and all the other day-to-day texts we encounter is a must-have skill set for our students. While these nonfiction texts may be dry, uninteresting, and lacking exciting plotlines or characters, nonfiction can also be truly fascinating, leading our students into intellectually invigorating adventures in history, philosophy, religion, nature, athletics, and so on. For all these reasons and more, nonfiction is an essential component of The Complete 4.

Reading and writing nonfiction generates an appreciation of expertise in our students. Introducing them at a very young age to writing and reading with expertise in a subject area builds their confidence and capacity as they enter into the world of research, which is hugely important when you begin asking them to research topics about which they initially have very little knowledge. They come to understand that other writers who are offering them information have their own areas of interest and expertise, and as readers of nonfiction we

draw on all of these when we find a new recipe, research the Civil War for a project, or help a friend who is ill find possible solutions to his problem.

The writer Grace Paley once said, "You write about what you don't know about what you know." I think this is very important to keep in mind as you create units in nonfiction. I do not want your teaching to be solely about helping your students find their "expertise" and retell it. I want you to help your students find both their preexisting knowledge and also find their points of interest and inquiry. Effective readers and writers have both ideas and questions, always. A unit in nonfiction highlights this point and gives you the opportunity through your own modeling to demonstrate it.

Here is a sample unit on nonfiction. Given the importance of the two types of nonfiction (informational and persuasive), I have included materials for both:

Name of Genre Unit	K–2 Genre Unit	3–5 Genre Unit
Nonfiction	**Informational:** • Students will read a variety of texts about one topic they want to know more about; for example, for students and teacher who are interested in weather—together they might collect *Down Comes the Rain* by Franklyn Branley, *Wild, Wet and Windy* by Claire Llewellyn, *Wacky Weather* by John Malam, and *I Face the Wind* by Vicki Cobb. • Students will notice characteristics of informational writing, including organization, chronology, Q & A, graphic aids, and text features. • Students will notice the connections between pictures and texts, and page layout and text ideas. • Students will research independent topics using simple strategies including webbing, asking questions, and basic note-taking; students will also read and write how-to books and become familiar with books that teach us things, such as *How Mountains Are Made* by Kathleen Weidner Zoehfeld, *How We Learned the Earth Is Round* by Patricia Lauber, *From Seed to Plant* by Gail Gibbons, *How a Book Is Made* by Aliki, and *How to Be a Friend* by Laurie and Marc Brown. • Students will notice that there is a balance of fact and explanation and cause and effect, and that photos or illustrations help explain a difficult idea or steps.	**Informational:** • Students will locate information across multiple texts and recognize and use organizational features such as contents, indexes, and headings. • Students will develop questions based on their reading and formulate big ideas using the facts they collect to bolster their big ideas. • Students will write a strong introduction to informational nonfiction that conveys their big ideas and sets the reader up clearly for what is to come. • Students will be able to identify what belongs in a strong piece of explanatory writing.

Name of Genre Unit	K–2 Genre Unit	3–5 Genre Unit
Nonfiction	**Persuasive:** • Students will write book blurbs and simple book reviews that state a point of view for or against aspects of the book they have read or the author they are reviewing. • Students will write to a familiar audience, such as friends, relatives, teachers, principals, or parents, in a persuasive manner about a topic that is of strong interest (i.e., revising playground rules, better food on the cafeteria menu). • Students will read each other's letters and simple book blurbs on the back of their own books written by other students; students will read teacher models of persuasive writing.	**Persuasive:** • Students will read and write more complex book reviews; magazines such as *New Moon* and *The Horn Book* provide excellent examples of anchor texts for upper-grade students in this area. • Students will read and write book reviews with a critical lens so that even if they like the book, there may be aspects of it they want to critique. • Students will write persuasively through the letter form and through the essay form; through the essay form, students will develop ideas and theories about texts angled toward character, theme, symbolism, or imagery. • Students will also pay special note to their reading of Internet materials to determine persuasive content versus informational content and factors of bias and unreliability.

As the chart demonstrates, even a brief introduction to this topic provides an abundance of teaching possibilities. Let me stress one more time that given nonfiction's relevance to life in the world after kids get out of school, and given that boys (who, studies show, are—across the country and in all social and economic demographics—suffering a "literacy gap" compared to girls at the same grade level) respond very enthusiastically to nonfiction texts, I recommend a heavy focus on nonfiction throughout every year from grade K through 5.

Standardized Tests

Standardized tests are one main key to opening important doors of educational opportunity for our students, from the time they are ten into their adult years, whether it is a fourth-grade ELA exam, an SAT, or a GRE. Let's not be afraid to help our students do really, really well on these tests. Good teaching does not have to stand in conflict with this goal. We should be able to say that our students write well and read well, when faced with any container, whether it be a poem, a favorite story, or a test. I want my students to feel the excitement of sharpening a number 2 pencil, as if they are going out to play in a big game—not as if they are about to be victimized by forces beyond their control.

The test, like the poem, has an author. A teacher's job is to create lessons that will help students understand the author's intent. This is not to say that a standardized test cannot throw a curveball once in a while. The poet Naomi Nye tells the story of how she received a copy of the Texas state exam in the mail, and it contained one of her poems. She tried to answer the questions about her own poem and got two of them wrong. One question was, "What do you think the poet intended?" That actually sounds like more than a curveball—more along the lines of a sandpaper-scuffed spitball. While that sort of question is just downright unfair, a question that is a little out of the ordinary or a little bit different is to be expected. So let's not let the curveballs get us down; let's instead do what we can do and make sure to give the kids the skills they need to be prepared for whatever the test throws at them.

I have made standardized tests one of the four main subcategories of genre study in an attempt to acknowledge head-on what everybody in teaching knows—no matter what almost every district in the country says about valuing teaching more than testing, and valuing genuine learning more than test-taking prowess—that there is enormous pressure on you as a teacher for your students to perform well on standardized tests. Enormous pressure.

The way to respond to that pressure is not to be dismissive of the test (reflects poor writing, wastes time, deprives children of time with their teachers to do some actual learning, takes teachers out of the classroom to grade the tests), but to acknowledge the reality and actually prepare your students for these tests through methods that benefit them as well by teaching them to be good readers and writers.

The best practitioners of any craft have the distinct ability to remain focused on what they are trying to accomplish; they focus on their goal and monitor their progress toward it. Your goal in working with your students in this unit is to prepare them to be ready for the test and to do well on the test.

One terrible trap that must be avoided at all costs is to forsake this goal of preparation to *succeed* and instead to simply prepare. The latter leads to lots of rote test prep, which does have the benefit of familiarizing students with what the test looks like, but which is devastating to their learning on many other levels. You can be creative in your standardized test units, providing your students with valuable instruction in literacy skills while preparing them well for standardized tests. By studying the test as a genre, we are helping our students hone reading and writing strategies to be fully prepared when they need their sharpened number 2s.

On the next page is an example of elements of a standardized test genre unit.

Name of Genre Unit	K–2 Genre Unit	3–5 Genre Unit
Standardized tests	• Students will engage in highly supported, playful practice writing in response to a prompt. • Students will read short, varied texts to get used to how it feels to switch genre in quick succession as they read. • Students may read magazines such as *Time for Kids*, *Click*, *Spider*, and *Ladybug* as examples of multitext reading, and ask what kinds of reading strategies help them make "quick shifts" as they read. • Students will be introduced to extremely basic norms and procedures of test-taking such as reading and following directions. • Students will practice looking at directions for games, puzzles, and recipes to practice good habits for direction reading. • Students will write directions for other students.	• Students must have the following qualities to do well on the test: content knowledge, stamina, speed, the ability to stay calm in stressful situations, time management, the capacity to shift their analytical mindset between genres, and a very clear awareness of exactly what they are being asked to do at each point in the test; this involves specific reading of instructions, as well as clarity of mind and focus, as they read through a passage about which they will have to answer questions. • Students will hone their skills in each of those areas. • Students will practice time-management exercises using excerpted parts of the test to build up their stamina and try to beat the clock. • Students will look at shared text on the SMART Board or overhead, which is in multigenre chunks, and discuss their metacognitive shifts as they move through the text from one genre to the next; the teacher will provide students with sample questions and ask them to clearly identify what the author of the question is looking for, and what kind of question the author is asking—i.e., an inference question, a fact-based question, or a story element question.

Name of Genre Unit	K–2 Genre Unit	3–5 Genre Unit
Standardized tests (*cont.*)		• Students will identify and name different types of questions; then they will practice these different types of questions in clusters. • Students will take two to three tests in succession as practice (much as when preparing for a marathon, the runner builds up for the big race) and receive their results. • Students will study them to determine which kinds of questions were the most challenging for them, and which require the most practice.

You can see that most elements of the standardized test genre study are applicable and beneficial to other areas of learning, both in literacy and other subject areas.

Grammar and Conventions: Vital and Meaningful

We want to integrate the teaching of conventions throughout the day, in the whole of our conversation with our students. The teaching of conventions must be explicit, but it also is so critical to effective reading and writing that we should integrate that focus wherever possible into all our teaching.

By building units of study that illuminate conventions, we are helping students forge a strong link between the drills they practice in their word-work time and the real experiences they are having as readers and writers interacting with text. For example, the first line of *Charlotte's Web* is probably one of the greatest lines in American literature in large part because E. B. White used his knowledge of dialogue and the tools of conventions to create an effective, multilayered sentence. The use of the tools of punctuation dramatically expands the meaning of the sentence and provides information about all aspects of the story— the character, the setting, and the plot—in one brief sentence: "'Where's Papa going with that ax?' said Fern to her mother as they were setting the table for breakfast." (Compare White's writing to a more common and ordinary opening: While Fern and her mother were setting the table for breakfast, Fern saw Papa go out of the house with an ax, and she wondered where he was going.)

We could learn about dialogue and quotation marks in drills and worksheets, but the best way is when we can call attention to these techniques in our explicit instruction in the teaching of reading and writing, and have students look for examples of grammar and punctuation to add to meaning in the texts they read independently.

Like the units in the three other Complete 4 categories, a grammar and conventions unit starts with whole-class instruction based on what we know about our students as learners. And then we provide daily regular opportunities for Independent Practice that connects the whole-group instruction to the work each student can do at his or her level. If we are using *Charlotte's Web* as a shared text to demonstrate dialogue marks, then each student will apply this learning to texts at his or her reading level during Independent Practice time. Miguel, a new English learner, might be searching for the use of dialogue marks in a second-level instructional reading book or an emergent playful picture book, while José, a more fluent English speaker, is searching for examples of effective use of dialogue marks in the book *Frindle* by Andrew Clements.

The example of Miguel and José offers a chance to stress my belief in two key elements of the teaching of conventions, elements that are critical to teaching in all other areas as well: 1) conventions are to be taught not as some secret code or rule book that the student must memorize by rote drilling, but rather as a living, breathing component of great reading and writing; and 2) conventions, like other lessons in the classroom, should be taught in a differentiated manner to students according to their ability in that area. So while both Miguel and José will be studying dialogue marks, they will be doing so using texts that are appropriate to their reading level and that will allow them to understand the point you are trying to teach—in this case, how dialogue marks affect text and meaning.

During opportunities for writing, students will practice the new skill they are studying and learning about by experimenting in their own work. Miguel might try basic dialogue in a fiction piece he is working on about his grandfather and magic, while José may use dialogue to represent flashbacks in a scene he recalls from when he was young in El Salvador.

Understanding a Conventions Unit

Conventions units may be categorized in the following four ways: studies of syntax, punctuation, parts of speech, and word study.

Convention studies are generally from four days to two weeks long. The spiraling of skills means that teachers will revisit areas of study with students across the grades, but, of course, with a different emphasis at each grade level.

Conventions are an area of teaching that really could use a burst of energy and excitement. It's always good to check in with yourself as a teacher by stopping to remember what it feels like to be a child, and the teaching of conventions especially benefits from such reflection. If you stop and think for a moment about the essence of the study of conventions, it can bring you back to what perhaps is lost in the recesses of our memory—how magical the realization that the symbols on the page can tell us a story in the same way that our mom's voice reading to us at bedtime can tell us a story.

The key with conventions is to try to help students understand that the symbols on the page are not a barrier to understanding, but are guides so students can understand the story just as though someone were reading it to them.

Syntax

If we accept that the purpose of conventions in reading and writing is to allow us to communicate through written symbols with the same effectiveness as if we were speaking directly to someone, then we see how syntax is critical. Syntax is the study of the rules governing the structure of language and the way the words are arranged to form sentences in a language. It is essential both to the formation of our story itself, whether written or verbal, and to the written communication of that story.

Here is a chart on a syntax study in a conventions unit:

Name of Conventions Unit	K–2 Conventions Unit	3–5 Conventions Unit
Syntax	• Students will study and become aware of and learn to apply spacing between words. • Students will become aware of and make use of the tenses of regular verbs. • Students will recognize run-on sentences and possibly fragments. • Students will learn to use pronouns when referring again to main characters. • Students will recognize and use subject, predicate, and object in their own writing.	• Students will recognize and write complex sentences. • Students will experiment with the tenses of regular verbs. • Students will recognize and use present perfect and past perfect tenses. • Students will recognize and use tenses of irregular verbs. • Students will know when to use contractions. • Students will recognize effective paragraphing and use it in their own writing where possible.

Facility with verb tenses obviously does not lessen as an area of study over the years. Instead, we focus on the complexity of the topic studied.

Punctuation

There is a certain joy and pride a young learner takes in working with the tools of punctuation. Like a big boy or a big girl, he or she is not only learning letters but special marks to put near the letters! I think that teaching our youngest students the rudiments of punctuation is one of those times in a classroom where we can set in motion very important conceptions in the child's mind regarding what school is like, what learning is like, what reading and writing are all about, and what sort of a learner the student is.

One main complaint against whole language is that it abandons the teaching of spelling and punctuation in favor of "feel-good" notions about getting a story on the page. "We need grammar," say parents. "We need spelling. We need punctuation." And so the pendulum swings back.

Rather than simply riding the pendulum back to sentence diagramming and drill sheets, let's stop for a moment and remember where the impetus behind whole language's aversion to focusing on spelling and punctuation came from. Imagine that you are just learning to write, to tell stories. You have some idea that markings on the page translate into words to tell your story. You are especially intrigued by special markings your teacher tells you about. These markings don't actually indicate that you should make a sound—they just help you figure out things about the marks that do make sounds. (Please stop for a moment and think, really, what a complex task we are asking our children to undertake in learning to read and write.)

With great relish, you put some symbols on a page and try out some of the markings your teacher has been telling you about. You proudly submit your work.

What you get back is a document laced with corrections, both in spelling and, even more dreadfully, in your overuse of periods. You thought you were being so diligent and clever with this new tool, and you have simply been exposed as someone who does not understand how to use the tool.

The educational leaders who developed the concept of whole language recoiled from this type of teaching; this is easy to understand and embrace. What is not easy to embrace, though, is a wholesale stepping away from teaching our children the critical communication skills embodied in the study of conventions.

And now the country returns to the old way of doing things, focusing on drills and worksheets. This is not the way to go.

Let us use our common sense and teach conventions as we teach other units: in encouraging, thoughtful, and engaging ways. A kindergartner I was working with fell in love with periods. She began using them after every word in the sentence. Big, bold, dark circles, overpowering the words. She loved the look of them.

Red scratches through all the extra periods would clearly not have been the best way to teach her. Besides squelching her exuberance, it would have the terrible effect of seeming to punish her for experimenting with her writing technique. On the other hand, we certainly want her to learn the purpose and proper use of a period. An effective conference would be to acknowledge and compliment her use and affection for punctuation marks, and indicate to her that there are many other marks out there she will soon be learning that are even more exciting, and then point out that a period really helps us as readers and writers because it tells us where the thought stops, where we should take a break in our reading. So support the child's love of periods, maybe encouraging her to draw a colorful picture of a bunch of them in art, but also advance her wonderful exploration of the use of periods by showing her how to use them only at the end of a sentence. In my conference with her on that day, I gently shared with her that I could help her to consider the rules for periods, so she would know where to put them. She beamed at me and said, "I think I know that rule, but I just LOVE periods!"

You can't beat that for a beautiful moment. (And less than a month later, she was using periods perfectly conventionally in her stories. I have to admit, I had a pang: I missed those bold, gigantic dots at the end of every word. The slipping away of childhood toward the conventional world—it is always a trade-off!)

Here is a punctuation study in conventions:

Name of Conventions Unit	K–2 Conventions Unit	3–5 Conventions Unit
Punctuation	• Students will recognize and use periods to end sentences. • Students will experiment with exclamation points, question marks, and commas in a list. • Students will recognize and use capital letters in the first word of sentences and proper nouns. • Students will recognize uses of colons, dashes, and ellipses.	• Students will recognize and apply uses of commas in more complex circumstances, such as dialogue and complex sentences. • Students will recognize and sometimes use punctuation for divided dialogue. • Students will recognize and use semicolons, colons, dashes, hyphens, apostrophes, parentheses, and ellipses.

The teaching of punctuation can seem to our students as though we are setting out arcane rules, solely designed to trip them up, especially in their writing. This obsession we sometimes have with correct grammar and punctuation, while wonderful in trying to create readers and writers skilled in communicating through proper use of norms for presenting the written word, also has a deleterious effect of making kids hesitant about experimenting in their writing. I think one reason children have always loved poetry units so much is that it is the one time when irregular or abnormal uses of structure and content in presenting the written word are actually encouraged and applauded.

I hope we can all use our teaching of punctuation to give our kids the technical skills they need to communicate effectively, but do so in a way that is interesting, innovative, and exciting. If we can teach our children that punctuation is a vehicle for enhancing expression, rather than a muffler that stops us from being creative in our expression, we will have worked wonders.

Parts of Speech

It is essential for students to be comfortable with both the names of the parts of speech and their uses. As with all our teaching in this area, let's try to make it as fun and drill-free as possible, but let's be sure our students are learning.

I hope you can tell by what I have said so far that I am very opposed to repetitive, drill-based instruction. I feel there are more interesting, compassionate, and effective ways to teach that in the end produce superior results in children's learning.

That said, I hope you also have gathered that I am deeply opposed to anyone dictating to a teacher how to teach in her classroom. It would be a ridiculous and sad irony if you were challenged in your use of a worksheet in your classroom by someone who claimed that a person like me, experienced enough at teaching to have written a book that seemed to make good sense, would not allow worksheets in the classroom.

My belief is that you should teach in your classroom in the way that works best for you and works best for your students. If you assess your classroom and determine that a drill practice is needed to achieve your teaching goal, do it. The Complete 4 (and my thinking) is supportive but flexible. Our teaching needs to be the same way: flexible when children need it, and more structured when they need that.

Here is a chart on parts of speech in a conventions unit:

Name of Conventions Unit	K–2 Conventions Unit	3–5 Conventions Unit
Parts of speech	• Students will recognize, name, and use the five major parts of speech—noun, verb, adjective, pronoun, adverb—experimenting with them in their own writing.	• Students will use, name, and recognize five major parts of speech—noun, verb, adjective, pronoun, and adverb—in more complicated sentence structures. • Students will recognize, name, and use prepositions and conjunctions. • Students will begin to incorporate a knowledge of relative pronouns into their writing in the upper grades (who, that, which, what), as well as compound personal pronouns (myself, themselves).

We see how the complexity of the study's topic increases through the grade levels, reinforcing and building on what comes before it.

Word Study

Take a look at the chart on page 71 in the K–2 column. I want to draw your attention to two words that are very intentionally part of the language in that box: "enjoy" and "playful." We are asked to ensure that our students are exposed to things like antonyms and homonyms in a way that is "playful," and that they "enjoy" exposure to simple derivatives.

What we are really doing here is embracing and pointing out the simple beauty of language. We read and write to communicate, but we really do so because it is so enjoyable to communicate. Words are meant to be used to tell our story to the world, so let's make that telling as enjoyable as possible.

Some of this teaching simply is dependent on your own love of words. As a teacher and a person, do you love the fact that some words are spelled differently but sound the same? Can you believe we have tolerated such an insane thing in our language for so long, with no apparent effort looming on the horizon to rectify such craziness? Think again of how things look through the eyes of the child: He sees the word *lead*. You tell him it sounds like "led," which is also a word. Or it can sound like "lead" with a long *e*. Same with *read*, which, by the way, sometimes sounds like "reed." Oy vay, the child must be thinking. Who invented this craziness!

For it is craziness, at some level. These rules are archaic, at many points. So let's just embrace it, making it active and fun. The world of words as presented through units on convention can be either one of appreciating all the incongruities and mastering them, or a world of mysterious rules lurking out there waiting to trap the student.

Our work with issues of reading and writing in our emergent learners can profoundly affect their view of school and themselves, so let's be especially careful at these ages in our teaching of conventions—but let's definitely do it!

On the next page is an example of a word-study unit.

Name of Conventions Unit	K–2 Conventions Unit	3–5 Conventions Unit
Word Study	• Students will learn basic dictionary use; will enjoy playful exposure to synonyms and antonyms, homophones and homonyms. • Students will also enjoy exposure to simple derivatives (word parts that come from another language). • Students will appreciate connections between word meanings in different languages.	• Students will develop a more sophisticated sense of the uses of a dictionary and a thesaurus. • Students will explore roots of words, derivatives, and language connections; students will recognize and use syllabication in their own writing. • Students will use style guides as a reference. • Students will recognize commonly misused words and expressions and learn their proper forms.

The incredibly rapid evolution of the Internet (as we addressed in the section on techno-literacy) sometimes seems to be threatening the very existence of dictionaries and thesauruses, as search engines can find definitions and synonyms faster than someone paging through a book. However, I would still strongly urge you to incorporate dictionary work into your children's studies. A dictionary is an amazing resource for much more than the simple definition of a word. It is also a place to find the meaning of an unfamiliar word as well as to see an amazing number of interesting words that you don't know!

Conventions as the Minor in Other Major Studies

Earlier in the book I mentioned the major/minor model of unit planning (and will explore it in more detail in Chapter 4). If you remember, in keeping with our model of the classroom and teaching as both organized and dynamic, I mentioned how we can think of majoring and minoring in certain units of study.

Conventions units are ideal as partner minors in a major unit in genre. There are some logical combinations, as you see here:

Examples of Convention Cycles Linked to Genre Studies

During narrative studies:	During nonfiction studies:	During poetry studies:
PUNCTUATION	SENTENCE SYNTAX	PARTS OF SPEECH
• Pausing punctuation—commas, semicolons, colons, dashes	• Run-ons, fragments	• Adjectives
• Dialogue punctuation	• Complex sentences	• Adverbs
• Possessive punctuation—apostrophes	• Paragraphing	• Active voice
• Elaborating punctuation—parentheses, hyphens	• Dependent and independent clauses	• Pronouns

Teaching conventions as a minor in this framework works very well because the content of the conventions unit ties in very nicely with what you are teaching in the major unit. This gives vibrancy and meaning to the conventions unit, much more than it would have without any sense of grounding.

The more we can help our kids understand that conventions are not simply there to torment them, but instead serve a very real and lively purpose in bringing words to life, the better off they'll be.

Strategies: Reading-Writing Synergy

Let's stop thinking of the teaching of reading and the teaching of writing as being two separate disciplines. Instead, let us find the synergy between the two. Ernest Hemingway was asked how to become a great writer, and he said: "Read *Anna Karenina*, read *Anna Karenina*, read *Anna Karenina*." The writer Ethan Canin said that in order to learn to be a writer, he kept a notebook as a young man and literally copied every one of his favorite novels word by word into it. The reading and writing experience is transactive and potentially transformational when seen as a combined experience. The skills are at their core exactly the same: finding meaning in written words. Whether you are creating the words or absorbing the words of another person, you are finding meaning in words. That is what we are trying to teach our children. That is our goal. That is what we must always focus on.

As soon as you accept that our job as teachers of language is to teach our children how to find and create meaning in words, the artificial breakdown in the teaching of reading and writing falls away. Your teaching practice in this area will not feel disjointed, or out of sorts, or (at its most distressing) nonsensical. You will have a touchstone for every plan, unit, lesson, and conference you will ever have with a student regarding reading and writing.

Understanding a Strategy Unit

Readers and writers employ strategies that help them make their way through tough texts, both those they are writing and those they are reading. Like anyone attempting any task they wish to do well, they plan, they think, they reflect, and then they act. Unsuccessful readers and writers neither strategize nor plan their writing. The biggest trouble readers face is when their reading feels unintentional. The same is true for writers, which is not to say that having a writing plan means being limited in creativity—even a writer who is free-thinking on the page can be working with an overall plan in mind.

Reading and writing strategies, when explicitly taught, provide our students with a toolbox to carry with them from one genre or one writing assignment to the next. Readers use strategies that include asking questions of a text, rereading to find meaning, and making active inferences as they read. Strong writers use similar strategies by asking questions of their own writing, making pictures in their mind as they write, and crafting ideas on the page that allow the reader to make inferences that aren't always so obvious.

Readers and writers also use organizational strategies to enhance their experience and the experience of their readers. For example, strong readers and writers have a very good sense of the text's organizational structure, and of revision, editing, and author's craft and are very conscious of these aspects of their reading and writing experience. They both acknowledge them as they read and make use of them as they write. For these readers and writers, revision and editing do not feel detached from the process, but are deeply connected and integral to the experience.

Whether unconsciously or consciously, readers use techniques for deepening thinking inside of books, and writers use techniques for deepening thinking on the page. They employ input and output strategies. For example, effective readers and effective writers deepen their thinking by asking questions. The questions should not be so specific that they address only one text or only one piece of writing, but should be broad enough to be easily applied in reading or writing in a wide variety of genres. Ask questions such as, What is the problem or conflict in this text? What lessons can we learn from this text? Which character has changed the most, or how are you going to help the character in your own writing change over time? What craft elements has this author used to hold the reader's attention? What craft elements have you used in your writing to hold the reader's attention?

The nice thing about framing a unit around a strategy concept is that while you can major in a strategy study, you can still minor in a genre. So the strategy of asking questions through text might be very different when paired with a nonfiction minor than it would be when paired with a fiction minor. In a strategy study in which we are thinking deeply about text by asking questions, our anchor texts might be *Walk Two Moons* by Sharon Creech along with *Hatchet* by Gary Paulson. The anchor question for *Walk Two Moons* might be this: What is the significance of Sal's journey? Then, in your students' Independent Practice, you might help them uncover the big questions: What journey is your character undertaking, and why?

In a strategy unit on thinking deeply about text through questions, with a minor in nonfiction, the anchor text might be *Look to the North* by Jean Craighead George. The anchor question could be this: How do animals take care of one another in the wild? Your students would then respond to the following question in their Independent Practice: How do the animals in your text take care of one another?

In a strategy unit, the read-aloud is a particularly important tool to use to model your thinking as you share the strategies that help you read and write with depth and discrimination. Strategy units anchored by a read-aloud help students write about and discuss theories about characters, relationships between characters and how they change, theories about how the book will resolve, metaphor and symbolism in places, people, and things; and purposes for certain sections, chapters, and events.

There are three main categories of strategy studies: input strategies, output strategies, and integration strategies.

Input strategies relate to comprehension. They include the following:

- Asking questions

- Making connections

- Making inferences

- Making sensory images

- Recognizing themes by connecting ideas

- Searching for themes and metaphors

- Critical analysis

- Identifying important and unimportant details

- Evaluating information, ideas, opinions, themes, and text

Output strategies relate to how we bring ideas to the page. They include the following:

- Considering deliberate organization of text

- Creating visual images on the page

- Forging text connections for the reader

- Building theme through connected ideas and symbols

- Using supporting details to bolster a thesis idea

- Making decisions regarding word choice and grammar that will affect the meaning of the text

Integration strategies relate to when a reader/writer is:

- inputting and outputting simultaneously

- thinking on the page to construct new ideas by contemporaneously generating output or connections based on immediate structured response to the outside source

Generally, this type of integration is done through a substantial kind of unit such as a character study, theme study, or author study, in which the reader/writer must operate back and forth between the two disciplines in a manner that requires him or her to be aware of and use both input and output strategies at the same time.

Let's take a look at the three categories in the chart below:

Name of Strategy Unit	K–2 Strategy Unit	3–5 Strategy Unit
Inferring (Input strategy)	• Students will make basic predictions; students will have hunches and ideas about characters. • Students will use pictures to develop ideas about story, or use pictures to develop factual understandings. • Students will name what good readers do to put together clues to form theories.	• Students will interpret facts from informational texts and from maps, graphs, and charts. • Students will make predictions and draw conclusions by linking characters and events in narrative texts. • Students will use specific evidence to develop ideas about characters, their actions, and motivations. • Students will identify the author's purpose and make connections to recurring themes; will ask penetrating questions that help form theories about themes.

Name of Strategy Unit	K–2 Strategy Unit	3–5 Strategy Unit
Organizational structures (Output strategy)	• Writers will write for audiences; students will be exposed to a variety of structures in which they can place their ideas, including basic poetry forms, how-to and expert books, a letter, an e-mail, and a friendly note.	• Writers will write for audiences; students will be exposed to an even greater variety of organizational structure in which they can place their ideas, including editorials, feature articles, more complex poetry structures, the essay form, longer letters, e-mail.

Name of Strategy Unit	K–2 Strategy Unit	3–5 Strategy Unit
Character analysis (Integration strategy)	• Students will discuss character attributes through read-aloud texts, especially where characters remain constant across multiple texts, such as Tacky the Penguin, Curious George, Big Anthony in Tomie DePaola's book, Frances in the Frances series by Russell Hoban, Frog and Toad, the Arthur books by Marc Brown. • Students will discuss the relationship of characters to each other. • Students will write brief character sketches inspired by the work they are doing in reading. • In their narrative writing, students will pay close attention to the character traits of the people they know or have invented and will practice writing about them.	• Students will examine inferred character traits and feelings, motivations, and decisions. • Students will study how we develop understanding of character—what characters say and do, what others say about them; what others do to them, things others notice about them, actions, dialogue. • Students will search in their writing for how characters change over time. • Students will write more extensive character profiles based on the work they have done looking at shared texts; their writing will include other characters' reactions to their character, and actions of the character that tell a great deal about the character without being overt; also, through their narrative writing, students will be able to show how in some cases characters change over time.

Name of Strategy Unit	K–2 Strategy Unit	3–5 Strategy Unit
Creating sensory images (Integration strategy)	• Students will practice building images in their minds as they read. • Students will use sticky notes and read-alouds to practice with the teacher sketching in response to their reading. • Turning to their writing, students will use sketching and drawing to help formulate powerful images on the page and will use words to match the images. • Students will use the genre of poetry to make reading and writing connections by acting out the images in poems, drawing in response to poems, and writing their own poems that reflect strong images that grow out of their observations and memories.	• Students will practice using read-alouds and shared texts to search for examples of powerful images in literature to use as models for their own writing. • Student will focus on fiction and nonfiction writing and learn how to create an image that will support a big idea—for example, if a student is writing an essay about the perils of cigarette smoking, a strong image paired with the big idea will help further the writer's intention • Students will read examples of nonfiction where the writer's thesis statement is bolstered by the use of strong resonant images; read-alouds with particular attention to strong image include *The Islander* by Cynthia Rylant, *Hatchet* by Gary Paulson, and *Bud, Not Buddy* by Christopher Paul Curtis.

Name of Strategy Unit	K–2 Strategy Unit	3–5 Strategy Unit
Author study (Integration strategy)	• Through a close study of an author, students will examine strategies writers use from text to text—everything from the ideas they choose to write about (such as Charlotte Zolotow, Tomie dePaola, and Donald Crews, all who write across genre, but who seem to draw on similar memories and wonderings from text to text) to their craft strategies. For example, Tomie dePaola plays with images of words, size of words, sound effects, and the relationship of words to picture; Charlotte Zolotow tends to use a lot of repetitive and poetic language to convey the essence of a strong emotion; writers such as Anne Rockwell and Lois Ehlert write nonfiction texts that are written in a crisp, clean, clear, and concise manner by using simple sentences and seeming to speak directly to the reader.	• Students will look more deeply to uncover the hidden themes of text in one author's body of work and to notice all the ways an author weaves themes from text to text, even when it is done subtly or not obviously. Authors such as Sandra Cisneros, J. K. Rowling, and Judy Blume reveal skillful use of story elements; students will read with attention to story elements, analyzing each one in these authors' texts and finding common threads. • In their writing, students will use output strategies to practice the kinds of craft elements they find in these writers' works, particularly those of external organizational structure, such as the crafting of a chapter or an essay, and also the internal structures, such as sentence length, repetition, word choice, and purposeful use of white space.

Now that we have explored each of the components of The Complete 4 in depth, let's begin to explore The Complete 4 in action by looking at the K–5 continuum.

CHAPTER 3

The Complete 4 Continuum

When you and your fellow teachers sit around the table in the faculty room, you have plenty to talk to one another about. There are the funny stories about your students, what you read this weekend, your own kids at home, your favorite television show, a new recipe. There are many ways in conversation we bridge divides, finding a sense of one another across a range of experience. Usually we tell stories to convey this kind of information and connectedness. But it is very rare to be given the opportunity to find authentic connectedness across the variety of grades within which we teach.

Typically, when we are given the opportunity to meet collegially, we meet with our grade-level team. These colleagues are sharing a more specific experience with us, and it is easy to connect with them in those ways. We share lesson ideas, and the joys and the frustrations of that particular age group. Yet, although this conversation provides us with the potential for much food for thought, we are doing ourselves and our kids a disservice if we do not try to find ways for us to talk and plan across grade levels. The administration must support this effort as well.

In this chapter, I am going to give you suggestions for the kinds of questions you will want to ask yourselves in cross-grade conversations regarding the teaching of reading and writing, and I will also share with you examples of the continua my team and I have written to help us have these conversations with teachers and plan as wisely as possible.

A continuum is a plan for what we want our students to learn as they proceed from kindergarten through fifth grade. I am aware that perhaps most of you will not have cross-grade continua in place in your districts as you read this book. However, I have included this section here because the process of creating a cross-grade curriculum is very much like the process of creating your own yearlong plan for the teaching of reading and writing. By being aware of these big-picture concerns, your own yearlong planning will inevitably be more powerful.

A continuum is what we create when we want to be able to see the growth of our students across time, using concrete, specific ways to mark their growth and plan forward. You will see by my examples that the continua help us in a big way to frame our yearlong calendars and make decisions about what we will teach in each year. They also help us in other significant, more specific ways as well: we can plan units with focus, units that are angled toward the outcomes we want for that particular year.

For example, we know we should teach nonfiction reading and writing every year. But the key is to refine the angle of our teaching so that every year has additional depth to it, and connects to the ones before it and the ones that come after. In kindergarten, we want to introduce our students to the features of nonfiction texts. Of course, we will always revisit this conversation from year to year. What we do not want, however, is for this focus on one aspect of nonfiction to be somewhat randomly the focus for your unit of nonfiction study *every year*. We expect your children to grow with intention across the years.

You have to have a sense of what your place is in this work: you are one important stop along the continuum. What is your part? Take a look at how we might angle our teaching in a unit on nonfiction:

Grade	Nonfiction Reading Focus
K	Becoming a reader of nonfiction
1	Understanding the difference between nonfiction and fiction
2	Reading nonfiction in search of answers
3	Using text features and graphic aids effectively
4	Making inferences and drawing conclusions in nonfiction
5	Identifying and validating fact, opinion, and bias in nonfiction

The children in our lives are passing through. Their journeys are just beginning, and we are their cheerleaders, their champions, their coaches, at the moment in time when we meet them. We get to know our own grade level really well, and it becomes part of who *we* are, too. When I work with second-grade teachers, I feel a certain vibe from them that reflects this time in children's lives: Children's reading is exploding; many of them are beginning to dig into chapter books and feeling the power of that. They are fast outgrowing their clothing, even by the day. They are able to think at higher levels cognitively but may still be sucking their thumbs to fall asleep. They are most definitely still gravitating to the dress-up box at home, but may be wearing more grown-up clothes to school. You, teachers at this grade level, have a finely tuned understanding of this age, and you are protective of their need to be inside the magic and vulnerability of their childhoods, while at the same time you know you can push them to write a lot on a page, or to read through to finish an entire series.

Meanwhile, the fourth-grade teacher is well aware of the intense social worlds swirling around the lives of fourth graders. They are exploring and making sense of the meaning and transient nature of friendship, and some of this plays out in the classroom. You know that this has to be recognized and utilized in your classrooms. You also know that your students are far more cognizant of the pressures of the outside world, of standardized tests, of parents at home, and so you are doing what you can to minimize that pressure. At the same time you know you can get fourth graders to do incredible things in their writing and reading. They can read complicated text and talk about higher-level thinking ideas, such as theme and changes in character. In their writing, they are much more able to manage and manipulate time as a strategy, not necessarily consistently, but nevertheless, they are capable of some higher-order thinking strategies, and the fourth-grade teacher wants to seize that opportunity and develop it.

Writing and enacting continua through conversation and strategic planning is essential if we are to make the best use of this knowledge base from which grade-level teachers have to write curriculum that is well suited to each developmental level. Doing so also provides a framework to integrate what teachers may feel they should or want to teach, despite uncertainty about how their teaching threads together as part of the child's entire learning journey.

Similar to generations passing down stories and knowledge and family values, so too do our school communities greatly benefit from building continua together. I am providing some continua templates. By working together to create continua off these templates, you can set forth what you value in your community. You can take a close look at your state standards and see how they can help you and guide you along this learning. You can reach out to your colleagues for their expertise, and unite your school community with shared conversation and shared outcomes. So, just like those conversations that connect you deeply to one another through your lives, you can find one another across district, community, and schools and say, This is who we are and these are our children, across time.

Considerations for Creating Continua

1. What are the outcomes we expect for our students by the end of grade 5? Use The Complete 4 categories for reading and writing to brainstorm your objectives.

2. What do your state standards say about reading and writing expectations at each grade level? Categorize these as well into Complete 4 outcomes.

3. Now, work with your grade-level colleagues to determine what outcomes you want for your grade level.

4. Report to each other. What are the similarities? What are the differences? Where can you streamline and make your outcomes far more specific to create curriculum that is practical and hands-on?

5. Remember: You will use the continua as a guide. Make them simple, clear, free of jargon, and easy for everyone to understand.

6. Now, using The Complete 4 categories, select one strand of the teaching of reading and writing and start your thinking.

See the appendix for a helpful Continuum Planner.

Building Continua

Building continua together with your colleagues is a way to capture the spiraling forward motion in your students' learning lives. It is not only about placing your students along a continuum. This exercise is about placing your teaching along a continuum; by thinking about your grade level and how it fits in with the other grade levels, you can best plan your year inside a big picture frame for thinking. This exercise is well worth doing, even if in your particular circumstance you are not designing cross-grade curriculum but instead are designing the units of study you will be teaching throughout the year in your own classroom.

If you are planning with your colleagues across grade levels, one key consideration for building continua is to name a unit focus for each grade level. By doing this, you are zeroing in on the key concept in each unit at each grade level, so that even though you are teaching fiction or nonfiction each year, you will have a very strong sense of where you fit into the bigger picture of what your students should know by the end of that year. The second key consideration is to establish grade-level outcomes for each unit. What you expect from your second graders in terms of what they know and understand and can do as nonfiction readers and writers will be different from what you expect your fifth graders to know and to do. By establishing specific outcomes, you will articulate from grade to grade what you expect most students will be able to accomplish. Finally, the third consideration for building continua is to identify key anchor texts that support the teaching inside your unit focus. It is really wonderful to select books and other kinds of texts for units, but your lists can easily get out of control, and then you never really use any of the books you collect. By matching your anchor texts to your unit focus, you keep a very clear sense of the connection between your teachable read-alouds and your lessons.

Let's take a look at each of these key considerations in greater detail:

1. **Naming a grade-gevel unit focus.** These conversations among your grade-level colleagues can and should be rich and full of excitement. Of course there will have to be some consensus building, but you should feel passionate about your unit focus decisions and enjoy creating them. I will share with you a sample snippet of a continuum in each of The Complete 4 categories so you can see how you might go about doing the same. Remember, your unit focus can be different from another school's unit focus at the same grade level, depending on your state standards, your community values, and your expectations for your children. Here are The Complete 4 samples:

Process: Stamina

Grade	Unit Focus
K	Lingering inside a book; lingering with a topic
1	Lengthening the amount of time a reader can be independent with a set of books; lengthening the amount of time a writer can be independent in a genre or with an idea
2	Setting goals for reading and writing longer, stronger, and faster
3	Using known structures (i.e., series books) to strengthen comprehension and build speed; using known structures to write fluently and with confidence
4	Reading and writing longer texts; sustaining time and concentration
5	Sustaining big ideas over time

Genre: Narrative

Grade	Unit Focus
K	Storytelling as rehearsal for story writing and retelling
1	Beginning, middle, and end—building a story sequence
2	Problem and solution
3	Character, setting, and the turning point
4	Theme
5	Point of view: perspective

Strategy: Theme Unit Focus

Grade	Unit Focus
K	Recognizing feelings and emotions as themes
1	Understanding that different books can carry similar feelings and ideas
2	Making inferences about characters helps us uncover themes
3	Finding evidence for theme through details in texts
4	Learning to create personal interpretations of text
5	Recognizing how different authors treat similar themes

Conventions: Punctuation

Grade	Unit Focus
K	Examining conventions writers use (directionality, spacing, some upper- and lowercase letters)
1	Investigating beginning and ending sentence signals
2	Exploring capitalization
3	Reading and writing dialogue
4	Understanding the comma and the compound sentence
5	Discovering new forms of pausing punctuation (the semicolon, the dash, the colon) in complex sentences

2. **Developing grade-level outcomes.** Using your state standards and your conversations with your cross-grade-level colleagues, balance your skills and strategies across the grade levels so that you can develop a set of common performance outcomes for each grade level and for each unit. I will show you a snippet of a narrative continuum so you can see the outcomes that were selected for each grade level based on these teachers' state standards.

Grade	Outcomes in a Narrative Unit
K	Draw or write original texts to create a story with beginning, middle, and end; orally tell or retell a story that contains the basic story elements.
1	Read and write fictional texts; use complete sentences in own writing.
2	Write original texts that have simple characters, plot, and setting. Recognize story elements in texts that are read.
3	Write original texts that have characters who use dialogue and show change or feeling. Read texts and be aware of change in characters.
4	Write original texts that demonstrate theme. Read with an awareness of theme.
5	Write original texts that deliberately use organizational structures. Read with an awareness of change in characters and the evidence from the texts that show it; read with an awareness of organizational structure.

3. **Establishing anchor texts.** If you take some time with your grade-level team and with your K–5 colleagues, you can identify key texts for each year and for each continuum, and then by fifth grade your children will leave your school with a well-rounded canon under their belts. (I am not saying, however, that a grade level should take possession of texts, or that no other grade level should have access to those texts. I am saying that by identifying key texts in each Complete 4 category, you have a systemic way to expose your students to a wide range of wonderful literature, and you can be sure they will leave your community fortified by their anchor text knowledge.) Anchor texts should really and truly reflect your unit focus, and not be randomly selected simply because you love them at a grade level. Those "must have, deeply loved" texts are welcome in all classrooms, as read-alouds and as part of the curriculum, but here, I am talking about texts that are integrally tied to your active teaching in units of study. If you do choose to use a common book title in more than one grade level, then you can use these books in different ways. For example, you might select *Swimmy* by Leo Lionni to demonstrate problem and solution in a second-grade unit focus in a narrative unit, and then you might use this same book again in fourth grade to demonstrate a unit focus in strategy for the theme study of cooperation.

Take a look at a snippet of a narrative continuum that demonstrates a selection of anchor texts for each unit at each grade level:

Grade	Anchor Text: Narrative
K	*The Mitten* by Jan Brett *A Boy, a Dog, and a Frog* by Mercer Mayer *Kitten's First Full Moon* by Kevin Henkes *Ernest and Celestine's Picnic* by Gabrielle Vincent
1	*Strega Nona* by Tomie dePaola *Shy Charles* by Rosemary Wells *Chrysanthemum* by Kevin Henkes *The Snowy Day* by Ezra Jack Keats *Knuffle Bunny* by Mo Willems
2	*Sylvester and the Magic Pebble* by William Steig *Swimmy* by Leo Lionni *Bedtime for Frances* by Russell Hoban
3	*The Night Eater* by Ana Juan *Doña Flor: A Tall Tale About a Giant Woman with a Great Big Heart* by Pat Mora *Whistling* by Elizabeth Partridge *Thunder Cake* by Patricia Polacco *Kamishibai Man* by Allen Say *Madeline* by Ludwig Bemelmans
4	*The Other Side* by Jacqueline Woodson *The Man Who Walked Between the Towers* by Mordicai Gerstein *The Three Questions* by Jon J. Muth *Fox* by Margaret Wild *The Stranger* by Chris Van Allsburg
5	*Bull Run* by Paul Fleischman *Zen Shorts* by Jon J. Muth *The View from Saturday* by E. L. Konigsburg *Zoom* by Istvan Banyai "Thank You, Ma'am" by Langston Hughes *Seedfolks* by Paul Fleischman

Now that we have taken a close look at each of the three key considerations, watch as I create a continuum by putting all the elements together: the unit focus, the outcomes, and the anchor texts. Voilà! A great recipe for a worthwhile cause! Here, then, is a sample of a complete narrative continuum:

Narrative Reading and Writing Continuum K–5

Grade	Unit Focus	Outcome	Anchor Texts
K	Storytelling as rehearsal for story writing and retelling in reading; introduction to story elements	• Draw or write original texts to create a story with beginning, middle, and end • Orally tell or retell a story with basic story elements • Draw a picture to represent a story • Use letters and/or words to tell a story	• *Corduroy* by Don Freeman • *Kitten's First Full Moon* by Kevin Henkes • *The Mitten* by Jan Brett • *A Boy, a Dog, and a Frog* by Mercer Mayer • *Ernest and Celestine's Picnic* by Gabrielle Vincent
1	Beginning, middle, and end: building story sequence and recognizing it in text	• Read and write fictional texts, using complete sentences in one's own writing • Use personal experiences and imagination to inspire writing	• *Strega Nona* by Tomie dePaola • *Shy Charles* by Rosemary Wells • *Chrysanthemum* by Kevin Henkes • *The Snowy Day* by Ezra Jack Keats • *Knuffle Bunny* by Mo Willems
2	Problem and solution	• Write original texts that have simple characters, plot, and setting • Recognize story elements in books that are read • Use descriptive language • Demonstrate organization and development • Identify problem and solution in reading • Identify use of magical elements in storytelling	• *Sylvester and the Magic Pebble* by William Steig • *Alexander and the Wind-Up Mouse* by Leo Lionni • *Swimmy* by Leo Lionni • *Bedtime for Frances* by Russell Hoban

Grade	Unit Focus	Outcome	Anchor Texts
3	Character, setting, and the turning point in story	• Write original texts that have characters who show feeling and use dialogue • Use descriptive, vivid language to describe setting • Identify problem/change in character, the importance of setting to the plot, and the turning point in plot	• *Whistling* by Elizabeth Partridge • *Thunder Cake* by Patricia Polacco • *The Night Eater* by Ana Juan • *Doña Flor: A Tall Tale About a Giant Woman with a Great Big Heart* by Pat Mora • *Kamishibai Man* by Allen Say • *Madeline* by Ludwig Bemelmans
4	Theme	• Produce imaginative stories that show insight into the internal thinking of a character • Create texts that demonstrate a strong theme and whose details support theme • Read texts with an attention to theme and its supporting details	• *The Other Side* by Jacqueline Woodson • *The Three Questions* by Jon J. Muth • *The Man Who Walked Between the Towers* by Mordicai Gerstein • *Fox* by Margaret Wild • *The Stranger* by Chris Van Allsburg
5	Point of view: perspective	• Write original literary texts that use organizing structures • Create a lead that attracts a reader's interest and is supported by the following text • Develop characters and establish a plot • Establish consistent point of view • Develop awareness of short-story structure; demonstrate character change • Understand that characters change; seek evidence in the text for how that happens, and why	• *Seedfolks* by Paul Fleischman • *Zen Shorts* by Jon J. Muth • *The View from Saturday* by E. L. Konigsburg • *Zoom* by Istvan Banyai • "Thank You, Ma'am," by Langston Hughes

The construction of a continuum is designed to help you plan your year, your unit, and your day. Now it is time to turn our attention to these containers of time.

Using The Complete 4 to Create a Year, a Unit, and a Day in the Teaching of Reading and Writing

In Part Two, we will take a close look at the three central time frames of our teaching: a year, a unit, and a day. Our challenge is that our teaching often loses focus because we are too reactive. We are reactive to our students, to our colleagues, to our mandates, and we end up reinventing our practice each year. We hear about genre units and we adopt them, often finding they become too long and too unwieldy, and we are never entirely sure what the outcomes should be. We know that our students need help in building stamina and fluency, and that we love to get them talking to each other in rich ways about text, but we find that these goals often get buried in the midst of longer genre units or content area units.

In the past 20 years, we have moved away from teaching grammar and conventions explicitly, but we feel a sense of longing for the days we remember as children when our teachers actually shared some of the rules of language with us. While we also treasure the freedom of poetry, how do we incorporate all we wish to teach into a coherent whole? The Complete 4 system helps you construct units of time that vary in length and vary in focus but that are systemic and organized. These chapters will unfold for you the three elements of time—a year, a unit, and a day—through the lens of the four components.

By planning your year and each unit with attention to the balance of the four components, we can create specific focal points and concrete outcomes for each chunk of time.

All good teaching at its heart moves over time toward a desired destination. Each specific moment of teaching cannot be preplanned, but planning for the short, medium, and long term ensures that the magic of teaching will occur, and will occur regularly.

In the last chapter of *Mary Poppins*, it is the first day of Spring. A West Wind blows in, and the children realize that Mary Poppins had said she would stay only until the West Wind came. Their time with a true teacher coming to an end, the children watch as "the Wind with a wild cry, slipped under the umbrella, pressing it upwards as though trying to force it out of Mary Poppins' hand. And that, apparently, was what the wind wanted her to do, for presently it lifted the umbrella higher in the air and Mary Poppins from the ground." The children cry. Later, they receive a package. There is a note from Mary Poppins in which she says to them, "Au revoir," which, they realize, means to Meet Again. "Michael gave a long sigh of relief. 'That's alright,' he said shakily, 'she always does what she says she will.'"

Unlike Mary Poppins, most of us will not be together again with our students once they leave our classrooms, but our teaching will always be with them. In this way, your "au revoir" is all the ways your teaching will circle back to remind them of that year in your room.

Unit planning gives us the opportunity to make commitments to our teaching and to help students make commitments to their learning. Situating a day of teaching inside a unit of learning will, I hope, make your teaching life a lot more manageable. Journey with me now inside a year, a unit, and a day in The Complete 4 classroom.

CHAPTER 4

A Year in the Teaching of Reading and Writing

Planning a year in the teaching of reading and writing requires both a dream and the details that go along with it, together with a positive but realistic understanding of the (hopefully) healthy constraints that are placed on your teaching. Similarly, good writing is about the big idea or the dream, and the details that play toward this big idea. The constraints placed on our big ideas in print are the consideration of our audience and the conventions of the English language, both of which are critical to good writing outcomes and in no way stifle a good writer. In fact, the more a writer knows about constraints, the stronger he or she is as a writer because she can use those constraints to her benefit.

She is empowered by her knowledge and understanding of the constraints and the reasons for them.

In our teaching, we can choose to be victimized by the constraints imposed upon us, or we can say, "How can I use these constraints to further my teaching?" So, for example, let me look closely at my state standards and assessments to see what they are saying, which will inform my instruction, and in fact help me plan and pare down what I have to do in my classroom. Instead of saying that the constraints are burdensome and add so much more to our teaching obligations, we might say, "How can these constraints release me from all the extras I have imposed on myself?"

We must have big ideas for our students, and also a handle on the details that will lead our students toward the big ideas, which will function as the building blocks toward our key understandings. Your planning will begin with your attention to big ideas. The details are the lessons inside of units you will build that will carry you toward your goals.

Questions to Ask as You Plan Your Year

As you plan your year, consider the following:

- What do I want my children to be able to do as readers and writers by the end of this year?

- How can I plan units of study with attention to variety in length, to keep my students' energy high for their learning?

- How can I make strong reading and writing connections for my students?

- How can I connect my content area work to the work we are doing in reading and writing, and have my reading and writing instruction move my content area instruction forward?

- How can I attend to the challenges of formal assessments by integrating the outcomes I want for them into my units? Or at times, as units unto themselves?

- How can I use my state standards to help me plan my instruction so as to have a strong sense of the continuum of learning K–5?

See appendix for a helpful yearlong planner.

Including considerations for state assessments does not mean you must forsake your best teaching. There is good work you can do in helping prepare your students for tests that is a lot more significant than simply getting them ready to take that test. For example, you might consider developing units in critical thinking or writing in response to a prompt, or writing about reading, or reading in different genres to help students be well prepared in these areas.

These units will help your students become stronger, more effective readers and writers, but they will also directly assist your students in their preparedness for the state assessments, which indeed ask them to perform in these modes. For our older students, we may consider creating a unit in our Complete 4 genre category on the test itself to familiarize them with the features of the test, including how to read in multiple genres on a test as well as how to read fluently and with stamina to work through the exam.

Be aware of what other curriculum considerations are necessary and what the timing is for those. Your fourth-grade team may be very committed to a longtime tradition of leading a science fair or celebrating colonial times. You may want to consider planning a unit on "how-to" writing in advance of the science fair or developing a unit in nonfiction research in advance of your colonial exploration.

What Are Your State Standards Saying?

Always be especially cognizant of your state standards. In New York, for example, the ELA performance indicators for second grade show a great emphasis on character and understanding of character; therefore, a series study that uses Horrible Harry as an anchor, and in which students study character in self-selected independent reading at their own level, is very much aligned with the New York state standards.

Also in New York, students are asked to read and write for social interaction. The Complete 4 process units on lifting the level of book talk, or our Complete 4 genre unit on letter writing, will reflect and live up to the intent of that standard. In fourth grade, students must use specific evidence from stories to identify themes. From The Complete 4 we might select a theme study in picture books to align ourselves with the intent of the standards. Not every state has drafted standards that may satisfy us completely, but many states have written excellent standards. We are obligated to use them to drive our instruction, and they can serve as a useful and essential guide as we plan our year.

What Does Your School Ask You to Produce in the Way of Finished Products by the End of the School Year?

Some schools may require a specified amount of writing for a portfolio assessment. Others may ask for a benchmark reading/writing assessment. If you plan for those now, you will not feel overwhelmed at the end of the year when you are frantically pulling student samples or realizing you do not have all the samples your administration requires. You can prepare your year with the intention of creating some of the product outcomes you want, whether they are for a portfolio or a school-wide assessment.

Do Your Units Build on Each Other in Terms of Adding Knowledge and Developing Skills in Your Students Across the Year?

Structuring your units to work with and build upon each other over the course of the year leads to incredibly powerful and effective teaching. Try to be very deliberate in which units come first, and which come next. In an upper-grade classroom, I would teach a unit on note-taking before I would teach a unit on research reading and writing. I would teach a unit on stamina before I would teach a unit on thinking and talking across books.

For my primary students, I would place a unit on an introduction to the classroom library before I would teach an explicit unit on book choice. In a third-grade classroom, I might create an Introduction to Genre unit before I would delve into nonfiction with my students. In my second-grade classroom, I would create a unit on story elements before delving deeper, later in the year, in a longer unit on narrative.

What Is the Canon of Literature You Want Your Students Exposed to This Year?

Don't be afraid to discuss with your colleagues what texts you all most want your students to know about and recognize by the time they leave fifth grade. Why do we wait until high school to offer our students a canon of literature? This conversation will depend on the values of your district and also what your community feels is important. Ask yourselves questions such as these: Which authors feel most age appropriate and inspirational for your students? Which texts are most effective at conveying your teaching points at your grade level? Which authors and texts are just too good to miss? Don't assume that your students are being exposed to these authors at home. Well-planned units of study give us a powerful opportunity to embed anchor texts that will have a profound impact on our students' lives.

Overarching Goals in Planning a Year

Now that you have carefully considered your state standards, your school's expectations for your students, the literature you want to include, any continua that may be in place in your district, and the ways that your units will build on each other, you're ready to set your major goals for the school year.

Achieve Balance

I have already said that The Complete 4 model was developed in response to this issue of balance. An effective reader and writer embodies a combination of strengths from the four areas of process, genre, strategy, and conventions. When our teaching throughout the year represents only the teaching of genre, for example, this develops student understanding of only one part of what it means to be a reader and writer in the world. In addition, virtually all contemporary standardized tests are not only assessing students' understanding of the elements of genre, but also their ability to think critically in text. If you, as a teaching community, really appreciate the study of genre, you might want to consider renaming aspects of your genre study to reflect the more nuanced layers of learning you want to give your students to help them achieve a good balance.

For example, a fourth-grade teacher reads a great deal of fiction with her students. With knowledge of The Complete 4 and a sense of a continuum of learning, she may want to be more specific in how she names her teaching. Interpretation in Fiction, Reading Historical Fiction, or Character Study are all unit possibilities instead of the more broadly and more abstractly defined unit Fiction. I want you to name what you teach not just as a semantic exercise but as an exercise in professionalism: naming what we teach and how we teach gives us power. We are not waiting for others to name our experience. We are naming it for ourselves, and the naming becomes our curriculum: organic, real, and ours. The issue very often may be about renaming and refocusing. Not redoing, not inventing unit ideas out of thin air, but rather reenvisioning your focus or clarifying it.

Studies that you might have named broadly as Fiction, Fiction, then more Fiction, then Poetry, then Research, could instead be made much more specific and outcome oriented. They could be named as units of study on topics such as these: Series Books, Independence, Fiction, Partnerships, Nonfiction, Note-Taking, Reading Identity, and Research.

In many cases, our curriculum is driven solely by book titles. If your reading year comprises *Sarah, Plain and Tall, Stone Fox*, and so forth, consider renaming them inside The Complete 4, using these texts as anchors inside the units. Thus for example, *Stone Fox* becomes a character study. *Sarah, Plain and Tall* becomes a unit with a focus on book talk and building ideas inside books. *Mr. Popper's Penguins* illuminates the qualities and components of fiction or story elements. *Because of Winn Dixie* could be refocused to illuminate a more specific study of theme. Let's say your writing year currently features memoir, poetry, and non-fiction. Renaming and refocusing with an eye toward true balance for you and your students would allow you to have a year in which you begin with a unit on building a writing community, followed by poetry study, then a strategy study on organizational structures, then nonfiction, and then reflection

Variety in Length

Kids do not have the same stamina that adults have. When we don't have a time frame to our teaching, we tend to go on and on. One of my colleagues, Laurie Pastore, once said that we know kids are sponges, but they only hold so much water. We have to know our kids' saturation points, before they lose interest, focus, and energy. Just because months run in 30- or 31-day cycles does not mean our units have to run by the month—or even more than a month. We have all let our teaching run too long. Mainly this is because we feel our kids have not mastered what we want to teach. Remember that each of us and our students is a person in a continuum. If you thought you had to teach every unit to mastery, you would get through no more than one unit a year, and maybe not even that. Select one or two things you want your students to do as readers and writers, as opposed to fixing everything that you believe needs fixing. Also, make your writing outcomes for each unit shorter. Each unit does not have to have as its outcome a tome worthy of Herman Melville. Not only is it unnecessary, but lengthiness of outcome can get in the way of a clean, elegant product that will offer you more in the way of assessment.

For example, if you are studying grammar/conventions, your student outcomes may be a thoughtfully constructed sentence or a brief paragraph. The product, then, is tighter and more evocative of your focused teaching points, rather than a broad stroke. Let's say you are doing a unit of study on stamina. You might teach four lessons on reading for more minutes in a day or setting goals on how to get there. The reading product, then, in the upper grades could be a reading log of how many minutes students are able to read this week. In a primary classroom, the product could be a collection of three books in a basket that your students each select to demonstrate how they happily "stuck with" their texts. In a brief unit on conventions in both primary and upper-grade classrooms, we might revise a sentence in one week with attention to new and interesting punctuation. By interspersing longer units with shorter units, we keep our students' energy high.

Longer units could have more extensive products. For example, a four-week poetry unit can lead to a poetry anthology in which your students select three poems they have worked hard and long on, as well as three poems written by other poets they love, along with a reflection of why they love them. A unit of study at the end of the year on reflection may culminate in a longer writing project, looking back across the year as a reader and writer, and reflecting on one's challenges and successes. The year and the units throughout the year should have a rhythm that feels comfortable for you. Short, long, short. Or short, short, long, short. Not long, long, long, short, short, short. Our students respond very well to changes in energy. They intuitively understand that certain topics of study require deep thought and inquiry, whereas others have singular objectives. Additionally, building variety in the length of your units serves as tremendous support for your struggling readers and writers. The student who struggles in a four-week study may feel more success in a one-week study by being able to see her own progress more quickly and clearly.

Major/Minor Focus

Teachers often complain, and rightfully so, that there is little time to do everything. As a way to make the most of your time, and to organize it, consider thinking about grouping your lessons according to major and minor focal points. On the average, if your unit is 15 lessons long, your major represents about two out of three (here, about nine lessons) of the unit. The minor should come from another Complete 4 category so that even within a unit there is a sense of balance (breadth and depth, instructional diversity, variety).

So, for a class studying fiction as a major, the minor may be about making text connections, which is from the strategy category. Or, a class may be involved in a unit of study on punctuation as a major, and the minor in this unit might be on fiction. As students are engaged in Independent Practice and

looking for examples of artful punctuation in their independent reading books, the teacher also uses the opportunity to minor in story elements. The major and the minor strands will both lead to closure and commitment on the part of students in terms of what they have learned and what the outcomes will be. What is great about thinking inside majors and minors is that it really helps to knit together your year. The major in book clubs (a process unit) early in the year, for example, can later become the minor as we study historical fiction. We are still going to hold our students accountable for great talks in their book clubs, and a concrete chunk of our Focused Instruction will emphasize good book-club talk, but the majority of our lessons are on historical fiction (a genre study).

We can use the major/minor model as a way to weave anchor skills into our teaching that will be needed in the next unit or the unit after that. A major focus is highlighted in one unit and then becomes the tool used in the next unit, where you are illuminating a bigger task, of which this first skill is a component. For example, in a classroom, note-taking might be a major focus of study in November, and then in February it is a minor focus when we are doing content area research. In this way, the major/minor model helps you keep your longer units to a manageable length. Oftentimes, a research unit can get out of control, turning into a ten-week unit, because after you begin teaching it, and unravel all that your students do not know, you realize they do not have the skills necessary to do the larger task essential to the unit. Instead, with note-taking as a minor in this study, the more significant text-to-text connections can now become the major focus of your work.

In a primary classroom, you may want to major in book choice as a reading unit early on, with a minor in genre awareness. Then later in the year when you introduce your children to the differences between nonfiction and fiction as a genre study, the topic of genre awareness becomes a major, but your children have had some introduction to the concept.

Teachers often wonder where to fit conventions into the year's planning. It is helpful to consider what kinds of major/minors go really well together in terms of conventions. Take a look at the chart to the left to get an idea of how you can major in a genre and minor in a conventions strand in a way that feels connected and sensible as pairs.

Major	Minor
Narrative	Conventions: dialogue punctuation
Nonfiction	Conventions: the colon
Poetry	Syntax: word order
Test	Conventions: complex sentences

Major	Minor
Fiction	Stamina
Fiction	Partnerships
Fiction	Author study
Fiction	Story elements
Fiction	Pausing punctuation
Fiction	Dialogue

Some units, particularly the shorter ones, should not and do not have minors at all. Incorporating a minor would defuse the power of the major work in a shorter unit and defeat the purpose of a unit focus. However, there are plentiful opportunities in planning to pair major and minor work. A good rule of thumb is to know that when you do have a minor, it should comprise approximately 25 percent of your teaching in a unit. So if you have 20 lessons in a unit, you will have approximately five lessons in the minor category.

The major/minor model is a great tool for highlighting work you have done, or previewing work you will do later in the year. The chart to the left shows some possible minor pairs through the major of the genre of fiction.

Stagger and Parallel Your Units Throughout the Year

Your units should never exist in isolation to each other, both in terms of reading and writing instruction and also in your content areas. When planning a year, let's consider two ways to integrate our units:

- **Stagger.** Create units that are partners to each other but one beginning before the other—preparing the field for the next one, so to speak. Reading nonfiction as a unit is a precursor to writing nonfiction. These are staggered units. A one-week conventions unit on dialogue marks is intentionally set immediately before a narrative study. The staggering is deliberate, so one unit is foundational to the next.

- **Parallel.** Your days are very busy, and so are the lives of your students. Forging connections between reading and writing feels healthy and helps you and your students manage time and also enjoy it more. Some units seem like naturals as parallels. Sometimes it is as obvious as reading poetry and writing poetry, and sometimes it is a bit more subtle, such as doing a sentence study in the teaching of reading, while simultaneously in the teaching of writing doing a sentence study on the parts of a sentence and ways to make a sentence feel complete and beautiful. Studying fluency in both reading and writing at the same time makes a lot of sense. In reading, we study the habits of mind that we develop as we build our fluency in the texts we read. In a parallel writing unit, we talk to our students about how we can get smoother on the page as we write. Using the same skills and strategies, we talk across reading and writing, cementing connections.

Content Area Connections

If you are studying the Civil War in social studies, you can put Walt Whitman, who wrote during that time period, into the center of your poetry unit. Whitman's poetry reflects a strong sense of the times and the American spirit. By studying the Civil War simultaneously, your students will have a much stronger appreciation for this poetry in context. Similarly, by studying Walt Whitman, an authentic voice speaking eloquently from the era, your students will have a much better appreciation of the historical period. A first-grade class is studying snails in science. To complement the science unit, you might want to plan a process unit in writing on the power of observation. In writing, students may be observing everything from the shell of the snail to their sister's smile. In another primary classroom, the students study living things in January and examine what makes living things grow. A reflection unit in reading and writing, called How I Am Growing as a Reader and Writer is a lovely accompaniment. You can build common language across the disciplines.

Must-Haves in a Yearlong Plan

In The Complete 4 categories of process and strategy, there are three key threads that should be woven into your yearlong plan:

- Identity building
- Interpretation
- Collaboration

Each thread begins early in the year and cycles throughout the year, appearing under the guise of other units and other subjects, but still serving as an underlying force that carries your year along and helps you in your planning. For example, in the primary grades, the study of **identity** begins early. Here are examples of how this big idea might be revisited throughout the year:

- **Who am I as a reader?** (process unit on reading identity)
- **Who am I as a poet?** (poetry genre unit with a minor in process)
- **How am I someone whose writing can affect others?** (process unit on writing for an audience)
- **How am I changing? Who am I now, compared with who I was at the beginning of the year?** (process unit on reflection)

The thread of **collaboration** also begins early in the year:

- **How do we talk with each other?** (process unit on partnerships)
- **How do we talk with each other in groups about texts?** (process unit about book clubs)
- **How can we create writing projects together?** (process unit on writing clubs)

The thread of **interpretation** is a bit more subtle but extremely important. Here are examples of how it might run through the school year for **primary students**:

- **Retelling** is the first step toward interpreting ideas (strategy unit on retelling).
- Later, students **talk about text** and find the big ideas in them (process unit in text-talk).

For **older students**, interpretation also begins early. In writing, the lived experience becomes fuel for the writing on the page:

- **What does this experience say about who I am?** (strategy unit on metaphor with a minor in reflection)
- **What big idea is the author trying to put out into the world?** (strategy unit on theme)

How to Get Started Planning Your Complete Year

Effective curriculum planning offers students challenge, enjoyment, breadth, depth, a progression and differentiation of skills, and personal choice and expression. To create curriculum wisely and well, you must assess needs and realities: the setting of your school; your co-teachers; your students (demographics, test scores, parent values, state standards). In planning, you want to develop yearlong outcomes or goals that match the needs of your kids and recognize the continuum of their learning and personal growth. Your goal is to create at-a-glance curricular maps that will achieve yearlong outcomes.

In planning a year, consider non negotiables. Where do non negotiables come from?

- The values of a community
- Responsiveness to state standards, mandates, and assessment guides
- The vision of the administrative leadership
- The history of the school, which includes time-honored elements or studies that have had an emotional, social, or intellectual impact upon the school community
- The work that will create a true balance; fill a gap in the continuum of learning; or realign a curriculum that is top-heavy in genre, conventions, strategy, or process, or missing one or more of these essential components

Where should non negotiables *not* come from?

- A teacher with a strong, intimidating voice, who pushes an agenda that is not comfortable for others
- A reaction to state assessments and standards that comes from fear rather than responsiveness
- A lack of understanding in seeing curriculum not as organic but as static and fixed, incapable of being changed or altered because it has been "finished"

Healthy nonnegotiables have strong benefits to the community and are anchored in clear, legitimate reasons.

For instance, in one school, poetry units each year fueled connections and inspirations between the parent community and the students. Each spring the students cultivated a "poetry garden." At the end of the four-week unit, students and teachers from all grades hung their poems on the fence in front of the school on a city street. Passersby were encouraged to "pick a poem" on their way to work. This, then, became an essential unit for the school, one well worth incorporating each year into the curriculum.

In building individual units, how will these learning experiences be organized?

- Draft a framing question for each unit
- Consider the major/minor focus
- Identify assessments and times when assessments will be administered
- Name possible anchor texts
- Develop lessons for your Focused Instruction
- Identify a time frame for the unit; plan backward into unit stages; look for lesson strands to connect one lesson to another; allow for student work and experience to inform your instruction as the unit unfolds

Understanding Your Environment

Successful yearlong planning requires us to take into consideration the supports and constraints that exist in the school and in the larger culture of education. No matter how dedicated we are or how wise and thoughtful our lessons are, few of us succeed without a realistic appraisal of the aspects of our environment that will help and hinder us.

Macro-Constraints of State-Mandated Assessments and Standards

Macro-constraints: Let's take a close look at the New York state standards as a constraint that can help us plan a great year of teaching. Standard 2 requires that students write for literary response and expression. The grade-level standards help us see the spiral upward through the grades. Here is a chart detailing key elements of Standard 2 in grades K–5 in New York:

Grade	Standard 2 – Write for Literary Response and Expression
K	Students will draw or write original literary texts to create a story with a beginning, middle, and end, using pictures/drawings and some words, with assistance and create poems or jingles, using pictures/drawings and some words, with assistance. • Students should be able to draw or write to respond to text to express feelings about characters or events in a story; describe characters or events; list a sequence of events in a story, with assistance; and retell a story.
1	Students will develop original literary texts to create a story with a beginning, middle, and end, using words that can be understood by others and create poems or jingles, using words that can be understood by others. • Students should be able to write to respond to text to express feelings about characters or events in one or more stories; describe characters, settings, or events; list a sequence of events in a story; retell a story, using words; and identify the problem and solution in a simple story.
2	Students will develop original texts that create characters, simple plot and setting, with assistance; use rhythm and rhyme to create short poems and songs, with assistance; and use descriptive language. • Students should be able to write interpretive and responsive essays that identify title, author, illustrator; describe literary elements such as plot and character, with assistance; and express a personal response.
3	Students will develop original texts that contain characters, simple plot, and setting and use dialogue. • Students should be able to write interpretive and responsive essays that describe literary elements; express a personal response; describe themes, with assistance; and compare and contrast elements of texts, with assistance.
4	Students will develop original texts that use dialogue (to create short plays); use vivid and playful language; produce imaginative stories and personal narratives that show insight; write interpretive and responsive essays that describe literary elements, describe themes of literary texts, and compare and contrast elements of texts. • Students should be able to summarize the plot, with assistance; describe the characters and explain how they change, with assistance; describe the setting and recognize its importance to the story, with assistance; draw a conclusion about the work.
5	Students will develop original literary texts that use organizing structures; create a lead that attracts the reader's interest; provide a title that interests the reader; develop character and establish a plot; use examples of literary devices such as rhyme, rhythm, and simile; establish a consistent point of view (first or third person, with assistance); write interpretive essays that summarize the plot; describe characters and how they change; describe the setting and recognize its importance in the story; draw a conclusion about the work; interpret the impact of literary devices such as simile and personification; recognize the impact of rhythm and rhyme in poems; use resources such as themes from other texts and performances to plan and create literary texts.

Implications for Curriculum Planning

What these constraints tell us helps us plan with attention to the spiraling up of skills. We are not just going to teach the same skills every year. We must hold ourselves accountable to the differentiated outcomes at each grade level. Looking at the standards helps us do this.

We should always keep in mind the particular standards at each grade level as we design our units throughout the year. So, for example, in K–1, there is an emphasis on story elements and the parts of a story—that is, beginning, middle, and end. In grade 2, students need to be able to write narratives that include all story elements (with assistance). This is the first year in which readers are asked to create responses that use details from the story to support their understanding of text. Student interpretive and responsive essays should focus on plot, character, and personal connections. In thinking about a curriculum yearlong plan, then, we must be sure to include explicit instruction on a reading response that uses evidence from the text to support and demonstrate understanding.

In grade 3, teachers are asked to teach narrative with a focus on dialogue and description, and students must be able to write essays that describe themes (with assistance). Third graders should be writing in response to reading beyond the concrete details and events of the story. They are now being asked to talk about theme in addition to plot and character. Therefore, we must be sure in our unit planning to include explicit instruction on theme or on writing in response to reading that includes theme.

In grade 4, we are asked to teach narrative with a focus on dialogue and insight (the capacity to gain an accurate and intuitive understanding of a person or action); students should be reflective in their reading responses. The standards are asking us to be sure to provide opportunities for our students to respond deeply in writing in response to text. We have gone beyond summarizing (though of course students still must know how to do that), to more sophisticated responses that include change in character and a comparison of literary elements.

In grade 5, students are asked to write literary essays. The standards across many states illuminate the literary essay, so we must include explicit instruction on that form itself. Included in the standards in grade 5 is an emphasis on point of view. So we may include either a major or minor strand in one of our units on point of view. In fifth grade, we can see from the standards that there is a perceived shift away from the responsive and creative-writing component toward the interpretive.

The standards clearly show a cycling forward, where students begin in the early grades by practicing organizational structures and literary elements by using their personal experiences to stimulate their writing, and then later, there is a turn in the upper grades toward the text. This information is powerful grist for us as we develop our own yearlong plans, by helping us organize a systemic approach to how we teach upward through the grades.

Micro-Constraints in Your Building and Team

What are your teaching goals for this year? What do you want your students to know how to do? What do you love to teach? Intuitively, you know better than anyone what you really want your students to do by the end of the year. Your intuition comprises not just your gut feelings and experience but also what you know about your students and your teaching community. Every teaching and learning community is different, whether it is the circumstances of the community itself, the support and expectations of parents, the challenges and successes of the community, the vision of the school's leadership, and so on. You consider all these factors as you decide what you want to accomplish.

Your own special talents and interests also shape your planning. Maybe you have always loved teaching poetry. Your love of poetry will not be inhibited by the structuring. Instead, allow yourself the opportunity to construct a very meaningful poetry unit and then revisit it later in the year as a minor focus of another unit.

What are you currently doing in your teaching of reading and writing that you really like and think works well? This approach of initially focusing on what is really working in your teaching will enable you to lay out a comfortable structure for your year, and more important, will make clear where the gaps are. Ask yourself what you are already doing in the teaching of reading and writing, even if you do not yet categorize them as units. Now follow this exercise: Jot down notes and place them into the appropriate Complete 4 categories. Notice which categories feel a little slim, and use this information to begin challenging yourself to add explicit teaching time to your year that relates to the missing pieces of The Complete 4 categories.

In one school, for example, the teachers noticed that they were teaching narrative, nonfiction, and poetry, and the rest of the year their writing workshop was fairly open ended. In another school, the teachers noticed that they did a lot of work on the stages of the writing process, and a great deal of work on research and note-taking, but allowed themselves little time to frame a unit around genre. A third group of teachers taught conventions intensively throughout the year through their word-work time, and really valued it, but had not yet

thought of connecting it to their students' Independent Practice, and so their conventions work was very open ended and never seemed to have any closure. And finally, in a fourth school, teachers cherished authors, celebrated craft, and talked a lot about metaphor and simile, but, although their students could craft a really beautiful descriptive line, teachers had not done much thinking toward the big picture of what students would do with what they had learned, or contextualizing this across the bigger picture of writing itself. Nothing "stuck" with the writer across time. What all these teaching communities realized by categorizing and using The Complete 4 model was that there were gaps in their yearlong planning.

Yearlong Calendar Samples

To help you visualize the results of carefully considered yearlong planning, I will now share with you examples of reading and writing calendars for kindergarten through fifth grade. These calendars are constructed by teachers in schools and are based on their own nonnegotiables, as well as on their needs and goals and hopes and dreams for their students. I have given you two samples of each calendar, so you can see how teachers have taken The Complete 4 ideas and made them their own.

If you come now to these calendars and feel overwhelmed, saying, "I could not do this," or "This is not for me," please do not close this book. Instead, keep reading. I promise you that you can do this, and I promise the framework will make good sense to you. And it is at that moment of relief and recognition (I teach these things! I may not have named them yet as units, but this is what I teach!) that you are going to begin to construct your own curriculum using these calendars as your guide, not as your mandate.

And don't let any particular deviation from a "normal" classroom time structure deter you from trying this. I was recently working with a kindergarten team that has a half-day program. To accommodate the compressed time frame of the day and their administrator's vision to incorporate science very explicitly, we created a very different kind of yearlong calendar. The units were completely parallel in reading, writing, play, and science. Focused Instruction in reading about Olivia, the title character in a book by Ian Falconer, connected to writing time, helped children develop strong characters in their storytelling. In playtime, the teacher began the session with, "You know how we are studying characters through our storytelling. When you go to your play today, be thinking about yourself as a storyteller. Who are the characters in your story today? When we come back, we will share some of your pretend." This team's members were well aware they would not have reading and writing time every day, but even on the off days, they were still reflecting back to the work of literacy in all kinds of integrated ways.

Feel completely free to use the calendars I share here in designing your own model. Follow them identically or create your own, tailored to your specific community. But know that the big idea here is that The Complete 4 creates true balance. The color coding will reflect that.

In viewing these calendars, you may choose to look only at your grade level. However, I strongly encourage you to take a look at the others as well. The more we can begin to talk across grade levels and become knowledgeable about other people's teaching too, the more benefits we bring to our students.

The ARCH

You will notice that the first month of every year in every grade begins with a unit called the ARCH. The ARCH is an acronym for Assessment/Routines/Choice/Healthy community. This acronym is designed to help you remember and plan for these four key ingredients in this first month, which lay the foundation for overarching goals and outcomes for the rest of the year. These components will of course look different at each grade level, so you will see in the calendars I have tried to show that spiral. But these four components do not change. Assessment is both formal and informal in reading and in writing. Routines are established through Focused Instruction and plenty of observation and reflection. Choice is modeled in terms of choosing both texts and ideas in writing. The Healthy community is established by celebrating reading and writing, and celebrating and valuing the readers and writers in your classroom through opportunities for talk about identity and about texts and ideas. To differentiate instruction grade by grade, I have created a continuum for the first month to share with you.

ARCH Articulation

Grade	Reading Unit Focus	Writing Unit Focus
K	Home/School Connections and First Steps	Home/School Connections and First Steps
1	Reading Role Models	Writing Role Models
2	Who Am I as a Reader?	Who Am I as a Writer?
3	Setting Personal Reading Goals	Setting Personal Writing Goals
4	Readers Think Across Books	Writers Are Influenced by Literature
5	Readers Consider How Words Change the World	Writers Consider How Their Words Change the World

The Four Prompts

Through my work in schools, I have found that you worry most about how children find writing ideas, and then also about what kinds of lessons you can do to inspire your students to mine their lives for ideas. I have developed a handy set of prompts in response to this concern; you will see that many of these samples contain a unit in the Four Prompts. Your school may decide to incorporate the Four Prompts into each year, or you may decide to integrate it as a minor into other units. The Four Prompts are: I remember, I wonder, I imagine, I observe. By teaching kids the Four Prompts, you will help them enter into their writing experiences fortified to make use of all they think about and dream about as part of their writing lives. I hope the Four Prompts will help you as you explore writing time with your students.

Calendar Samples

The following calendar samples are designed to help you move forward in planning. You may choose to *adopt* one of these, *adapt* one of them, or *create* your own, using the samples as guides.

Kindergarten Calendar—Sample One

PROCESS=red   GENRE=green   STRATEGY=orange   CONVENTIONS=blue

MONTH	READING UNITS	WRITING UNITS
Sept.	The ARCH: Home/School Connections and First Steps	The ARCH: Home/School Connections and First Steps
Oct.	Telling Stories Through Pictures, Using Fairy Tales or Folktales	Storytelling
Nov.	Welcome to the Library 1 week	Writing for Others (letters, signs, labels in play areas) 2 weeks
	Looking at Print With Label and List Books 2 weeks	Writing Words Without Worry (while making labeled stories) 1 week
Dec.	Partnerships 1 week	Partnerships 1 week
	Narrative 2 weeks	Narrative 2 weeks
Jan.	Refreshing Routines	Refreshing Routines
Feb.	Retelling Using Story Elements	Retelling as a Tool to Add to Stories
March	Nonfiction	Nonfiction 3 weeks
		Rules Writers Use (can be punctuation, capitalization, and/or spacing) 1 week
April	Reading With Phrasing and Fluency (using poetry and leveled texts) 2 weeks	Poetry 3 weeks
	Readers Enjoy Rhythm of Text (Poetry and Song) 2 weeks	Super Spellers (using spelling strategies and/or resources) 1 week
May	Fiction	Fiction
June	Summer Reading Plans	Summer Writing Plans

Kindergarten Calendar—Sample Two

MONTH	READING UNITS	WRITING UNITS
Sept.	The ARCH: Home/School Connections and First Steps	The ARCH: Home/School Connections and First Steps
Oct.	Introduction to Partnerships: Looking at Picture Books Together 2 weeks	The Four Prompts: Writers Remember, Wonder, Imagine, and Observe 2 weeks
	Telling Stories Through Pictures 2 weeks	Storytelling 2 weeks
Nov.	Elements of Story	Narrative: Writers Tell Stories From Their Lives
Dec.	Readers Have Passions and Read About Them	Writers Have Passions and Write About Them
Jan.	Reading Detectives: Developing Effective Word-Attack Strategies	Using Spelling Strategies 1 week
		Author Study 3 weeks
Feb.	What Is Nonfiction?	List and Label Books
March	Fluency Through Poetry and Song 2 weeks	An Introduction to Punctuation 2 weeks
	Poetry 2 weeks	Poetry 2 weeks
April	Readers Use Play to Retell Stories	Writers Use Play to Explore New Ideas
May	Reading and Responding to Fiction	Writing Fiction
June	Looking Back, Moving Ahead as a Reader	Looking Back, Moving Ahead as a Writer

Teaching/Learning Explanation: Kindergarten

Home/school connections are vitally important for kindergarten planning. So to make that part of your explicit instruction in the kindergarten curriculum, I have set up the year to incorporate ample opportunity for these connections. Your lessons will include opportunities to talk to students about the following:

Environment. What makes you comfortable as a reader at home? What makes you comfortable at school? With whom do you read at home? With whom do you read in school? What kinds of books do you read at home? What kinds of books do you read at school?

When my daughter came home from her first day of kindergarten, I asked her, "How did it go?" (with my heart in my throat, of course!). She said, "It was really great. I didn't think about you the whole time I was at recess." My eyes filled with tears at the thought of her having a moment of not missing home: at recess! We cannot underestimate the power of the home/school connection at this age. Let us make it part of the energy of our literacy instruction.

And for those students who are not receiving ample access to books or read-alouds at home, our instruction is a way for us to enhance student awareness so that when students take a book home from school, they will consider their favorite reading spot, or who will read to them at home, or whom they will want to read to at home.

Types of texts. It is funny that when children first come to kindergarten, the gulf between home and school seems so vast. At school the types of texts that are being read to them or the way they are being read may be very different from those they have seen or heard at home. The repetitive patterns and soothing rhythms of the texts that parents reach for at bedtime no longer seem front and center once students get to the classroom. Maybe this is partly because we don't want our kids to fall asleep, but maybe it is because we put a lot of pressure on ourselves to come up with something new and different. In fact, these familiar books have much to teach us about the way great literature is written and about learning to read.

Goodnight Moon by Margaret Wise Brown is brilliantly written, though deceptively simple. It is no surprise that generation after generation returns to it. This book would be a powerful anchor text for your kindergarten teaching. The rhythms of this text and the occasional rhymes are funny, unpredictable, sudden. The picture-to-text connections illuminate, surprise, and slyly delight.

Your work can go in both directions: home to school, and school to home. In other words, over the course of several of these units, students can bring in their favorite bedtime books to read during Independent Practice time and can share them with each other during partnerships. Conversely, your students can take home some of the texts you provide as part of your bedtime study to read at home with their families as "homework." If their parents don't read English, part of the work in this unit can be about taking picture walks, and your students can go home as "experts," becoming the "reader" at bedtime.

Possible units in kindergarten relate to conventions of print. In this year, we want to build ample opportunities to explicitly introduce our students to the tools of a reader's and writer's trade—not only the alphabet, of course, but the ways in which readers and writers put letters down together to formulate their thinking. You will note that I include several units relating to these toolbox skills. This work does not have to be onerous. Your children are young, and they love even the look of the alphabet letters. They are delightfully new to written language, so your explicit instruction can again integrate your major learning areas throughout your kindergarten day. For example, in a fluency unit in reading, your Focused Instruction might call your students' attention to a simple big-book text, using your voice to help the children hear how you read smoothly, and using picture cues to clue them in to the expression in your voice.

Your Focused Instruction in writing may call their attention to how they can go about using an alphabet chart, while, as a precursor to playtime, your Focused Instruction may be about giving your children sticky notes, index cards, and note pads to play with the sounds of language as they take notes in their pretend restaurant or make signs for their building in the block area.

Kindergarteners are most certainly not too young to reflect on their learning. Quite the opposite. They are studying themselves for signs of minute growth, from their sneaker size to their loose tooth to their letter formations. Take your time, and through explicit instruction, call their attention to what their learning has been.

In your Focused Instruction in reading during reflection units, ask your students to notice how they are using pictures to help tell a story, or what they have learned about nonfiction reading versus fiction reading, or what they now know about characters that they might not have known at the beginning of the year.

In your Focused Instruction in writing, you may be asking your students to notice how much more smoothly they can write on the page now, what punctuation marks they have learned, and what kinds of genres they have created this year.

In Focused Instruction as a precursor to play, you will angle the reflection back to literacy even there. You might say to your students, "I am noticing that you really sustained that story in the block area by building that castle over a few days' time. I saw you talking with your friends about what happens in that castle all these past few days." Or you might say, "I was really admiring how funny you were in the housekeeping corner as you pretended today. When you told us the story just now about what you did in housekeeping, it made us all laugh. You are a good storyteller."

When my daughters were young, they could make castles and ships out of our livingroom couch; and I knew that there on the couch they were flexing their muscles for storytelling, meaning making, metaphor building, and sustained narrative. Over the years, K–1 teachers have said to me many times that they often resist a more structured reading and writing approach because they feel that play gets lost, and play feels so essential to them as educators. I hear that, and I agree with that, and yet I don't want one to compromise the other, either. I believe children need structure for both reading and writing instruction, and also a way to feel that play connects to becoming a reader and a writer as much as anything else in the world does. For this reason, I include explicit units at both the Kindergarten and first-grade level where I connect play to literacy education. As students build in the block area, they are creating stories, and you can encourage them to build upon their stories as precursors to narratives they will later write during their Independent Practice time in writing. Students can bring note pads into the dramatic-play area or the kitchen area to record their conversations, to invent stories of what happens to their characters, or even to use these writing tools as props to their narratives.

Grade 1 Calendar—Sample One

MONTH	READING UNITS	WRITING UNITS
Sept.	The ARCH: Reading Role Models	The ARCH: Writing Role Models
Oct.	Using Reading Strategies: Word Attack, Comprehension, Book Choice	Using Writing Strategies: Spelling, Writing Ideas, Paper Choice
Nov.	Partnerships Through Poetry and Songs	The Four Prompts 3 weeks
		Poetry and Songs 1 week
Dec.	Phrasing and Fluency	Poetry and Songs
Jan.	Nonfiction	Fluency 1 week
		Nonfiction: How-To Books 3 weeks
Feb.	Noticing Punctuation 1 week	Nonfiction: How-To Books 2 weeks
	Readers Read With Passion About Their Interests 3 weeks	Using Punctuation to Change Our Writing 2 weeks
March	Story Elements 2 weeks	Narrative
	Retelling Partnerships 2 weeks	
April	Stamina and Independence 3 weeks	Stamina and Independence 3 weeks
	Reading the Word Wall and Noticing Word Patterns 1 week	Spelling Strategies 1 week
May	Character Clubs 2 weeks	Fiction With a Character Focus 3 weeks
	Deepening Book Talk Through Fiction 2 weeks	Revision 1 week
June	Looking Back, Looking Ahead: Summer Reading Plans	Looking Back, Looking Ahead: Summer Writing Plans

Grade 1 Calendar—Sample Two

PROCESS=red   GENRE=green   STRATEGY=orange   CONVENTIONS=blue

MONTH	READING UNITS	WRITING UNITS
Sept.	The ARCH: Reading Role Models	The ARCH: Writing Role Models
Oct.	Print Strategies 2 weeks	Print Strategies 2 weeks
	Partnerships 2 weeks	Partnerships 2 weeks
Nov.	Wise Book Choices 1 week	Rules Writers Use (capitals, lowercase, spacing, punctuation) 2 weeks
	Narrative (story elements and retelling) 3 weeks	Storytelling 2 weeks
Dec.	Readers Are Thinkers: Prediction	Narrative
Jan.	Readers Talk About Books in Partnerships 1 week	Author Study 3 weeks
	Character Clubs 3 weeks	Writing Long and Strong 1 week
Feb	Nonfiction	Nonfiction
March	Review of Print Strategies: Readers Revise and Reread 2 weeks	Nonfiction 1 week
	Readers Are Thinkers: Making Connections Across Genres 2 weeks	Writers as Thinkers: Trying Our Writing in a Variety of Genres 3 weeks
April	Fluency and Phrasing 2 weeks	Developing Writing Ideas: The Four Prompts 2 weeks
	Reading Stamina 2 weeks	Fluency and Conventions 2 weeks
May	Poetry	Poetry
June	Reflection and Assessment: How I Have Grown as a Reader	Reflection and Assessment: How I Have Grown as a Writer

Teaching/Learning Explanation: Grade 1

From first grade forward, you will notice that each subsequent year contains references or even a unit unto itself on The Four Prompts (I wonder/I remember/ I observe/I imagine). Teachers are always asking, "How can I get my students to find writing ideas?" I have seen teachers come up with myriad ways to do this. But I have found that by offering my students four basic prompts, they can use these to write the whole year long in any genre, in any modality. This enables you to teach writing as simply and directly as possible with the fewest complications.

Fluency plays a big role in the first-grade year. Talk to your students about how punctuation helps a reader read smoothly and comfortably. Talk to your readers and writers about how to read sentences as opposed to individual words. Through shared reading and writing experiences, demonstrate how sentences have their own structures, and are of varied length, affecting how we read and how our voice sounds, both in our heads and as we read aloud across a page.

First graders are joyous about their newfound skills. They are relishing that they can write a sentence, and read a longer book. Others in your classroom are still learning their alphabet letters; they are beginning to become aware of themselves in relation to others as readers and writers. There is a huge range in a first-grade classroom, as you well know. These units are designed to build collaboration: students can use partnerships to read aloud from their own writing to each other, or retell a written text as rehearsal for their own reading.

First graders are curious about the world and about making connections. They will see connections everywhere! And even though they may still wait for the tooth fairy, they can help their baby sister get dressed. They are small and big all at the same time. For this reason, I have built yearlong calendars with teachers for this grade level that are deeply scaffolded: lots of opportunities to "practice" everything: from book choice, to how you sit with a partner, to reading aloud. And at the same time, I have incorporated opportunities to build independence through longer nonfiction units and introduction to story elements.

Nick DeMillo

Grade 2 Calendar — Sample One

PROCESS=red   GENRE=green   STRATEGY=orange   CONVENTIONS=blue

MONTH	READING UNITS	WRITING UNITS
Sept.	The ARCH: Who Am I as a Reader?	The ARCH: Who Am I as a Writer?
Oct.	Fluency and Punctuation 1 week Readers Share Favorite Books With Others 3 weeks	The Four Prompts 3 weeks Fluency and Punctuation 1 week
Nov.	Character Study	Writing Letters: Developing a Sense of Audience
Dec.	Dialogue Study 1 week Series Book Partnerships 2 weeks	Character Study 2 weeks The Comma 1 week
Jan.	Series Books: Making Connections	Book Blurbs: Writing About Reading
Feb.	Reading Nonfiction in Search of Answers	Nonfiction: Research Beginnings
March	Readers Read With Passion About Topics of Interest to Them	Writing Clubs
April	Studying the Sentence 1 week Genre Clubs 3 weeks	Sentence Structure 1 week Stamina and Independence 3 weeks
May	Poetry	Poetry
June	Looking Back, Looking Ahead: Summer Reading Plans	Looking Back, Looking Ahead: Summer Writing Plans

Grade 2 Calendar—Sample Two

PROCESS=red   GENRE=green   STRATEGY=orange   CONVENTIONS=blue

MONTH	READING UNITS	WRITING UNITS
Sept.	The ARCH: Who Am I as a Reader?	The ARCH: Who Am I as a Writer?
Oct.	Readers Make Wise Book Choices 2 weeks	Writers Make Choices 2 weeks
	Stamina 2 weeks	Stamina 2 weeks
Nov.	Readers Are Thinkers: Inferring 3 weeks	Rules Writers Use 2 weeks
	Decoding Strategies for Challenging Words 1 week	Author Study 2 weeks
Dec.	Series Books	Fiction
Jan.	Character Clubs	The Four Prompts 2 weeks
		Comparing Characters 2 weeks
Feb.	Content Area Connections: Nonfiction	Nonfiction
March	Review of Print Strategies: Readers Revise and Reread 2 weeks	Syntax 1 week
	Readers Are Thinkers: Making Connections Across Genres 2 weeks	Writers Make Plans: Thinking, Dreaming, Creating Writing Projects 3 weeks
April	Text Clubs: Building Conversations	Writing About Reading: Book Blurbs 3 weeks
		Paragraphing 1 week
May	Poetry 2 weeks	Poetry
	Fluency 2 weeks	
June	Reflection and Assessment: How I Have Grown as a Reader	Reflection and Assessment: How I Have Grown as a Writer

Teaching/Learning Explanation: Grade 2

Note that the first unit in each year K–2 spirals upward, just as genre units do. This unit is always a process unit in the primary grades. All the units at each grade level will help you create community and impart to your students just how important reading and writing will be this year. The kindergartner learns about being part of a community by having connections made between home and school. The first grader learns how a community of writers and readers is formed by building off that first year of home/school connections and looking around his or her local community or school for reading and writing role models. In the second-grade year, your students are prepared for more reflection and identity building of their own reading and writing experience, and it is at this point that we can ask the questions, "Who am I as a writer? Who am I as a reader? How will I grow and change this year?"

Readers and writers in second grade should have a growing awareness of the uses and complexities of story elements. Therefore, I have included significant time for the study of character in both reading and writing. Note as well that I reserve time for series books in reading and a connected theme study in writing. Children in this year gravitate toward series books because their fluency is building; their comfort with text is deepening. And yet, they still want to feel safe inside a known entity. Series books are meant to be predictable. They are designed for the reader who wants a comfortable experience. With series books as a foundation, you can springboard off into conversations about character and theme, using texts that feel immensely readable, satisfying, and not too risky for your students.

Second grade is a big year. Your students are coming into their own, both inside and outside of school. They admire the older kids for their independence and want to be just like them. And yet, at home they may still curl up with mom or dad and want their bedtime snuggles. They are able to read longer texts, but still may need lots of support to hold on to the big ideas in a story. Like their beautiful faces, which reflect both growth and the babies they once were, their writing is perhaps nearly conventional but still full of potential for moving closer to conventional along the continuum. Therefore, the mini-units in conventions will be deeply helpful to them as they continue their forays into the world of larger audiences for their writing, and to share their writing with others.

Grade 3 Calendar—Sample One

PROCESS=red   GENRE=green   STRATEGY=orange   CONVENTIONS=blue

MONTH	READING UNITS	WRITING UNITS
Sept.	The ARCH: Setting Personal Reading Goals	The ARCH: Setting Personal Writing Goals
Oct.	Complex Sentences 1 week	The Four Prompts 3 weeks
	Fiction 3 weeks	Sentence Variety 1 week
Nov.	Techno-literacy 1 week	Techno-literacy: Writing E-mails 2 weeks
	Accessing Information in Nonfiction Texts 3 weeks	Nonfiction Wonderings 2 weeks
Dec.	Punctuation 2 weeks	Rereading to Edit Writing 1 week
	Reading the Test 2 weeks	Crafting Responses to Test Questions 3 weeks
Jan.	Exploring Reading Interests	Exploring Writing Interests
Feb.	Exploring Theme Through Picture Books	Narrative: Writers Write From Their Lives and From Their Imaginations
March	Text Talks: Partnerships	Writing Partnerships 3 weeks
		Rereading and Revising for Audience 1 week
April	Poetry 3 weeks	Parts of Speech: The Verb and the Adjective 1 week
	Noticing and Admiring Authors' Word Choice 1 week	Poetry 3 weeks
May	Genre Clubs	Book Reviews
June	Looking Back, Looking Ahead: Summer Reading Plans	Looking Back, Looking Ahead: Summer Writing Plans

Grade 3 Calendar—Sample Two

PROCESS=red   GENRE=green   STRATEGY=orange   CONVENTIONS=blue

MONTH	READING UNITS	WRITING UNITS
Sept.	The ARCH: Setting Personal Reading Goals	The ARCH: Setting Personal Writing Goals 3 weeks
		The Four Prompts 1 week
Oct.	Story Elements 1 week	Partnership Study Using Stories 2 weeks
	Partnership Study Using Series Books 3 weeks	Narratives From Our Lives and From Our Imaginations 2 weeks
Nov.	Deducing Meaning of Unknown Words: Word Study 1 week	Sentence Study 2 weeks
	Nonfiction Text Supports 3 weeks	Note-Taking 2 weeks
Dec.	Test Preparation	Complex Sentences 1 week
		Test Preparation 3 weeks
Jan.	Author Studies 2 weeks	Writing Clubs 2 weeks
	Techno-literacy 2 weeks	Writing About Reading: Theme 2 weeks
Feb.	Text Clubs: Building Conversations	Crafting E-mails to Convey Ideas 2 weeks
		Punctuation 2 weeks
March	Nonfiction in the Content Areas	Nonfiction in the Content Areas
April	Building Vocabulary: Vivid Verbs and Awesome Adjectives 2 weeks	Building Vocabulary: Vivid Verbs and Awesome Adjectives 1 week
	Poetry 2 weeks	Poetry 3 weeks
May	Theme	Building Themes Inside Picture Books
June	Reflection and Assessment: How I Have Grown as a Reader	Reflection and Assessment: How I Have Grown as a Writer

Teaching/Learning Explanation: Grade 3

In the third-grade year, there is a newly emphasized, fruitful emphasis on writing about reading. Through nonfiction reading as well as through the ever-present series books, your students are learning to respond to text in a variety of ways and with a variety of texts. Forms of writing about reading come to the fore in this year, and your students are ready for them. They include book reviews and a short, manageable introduction to the essay form. Inspired by the national call for standardized assessment beginning at the third-grade level, and its emphasis on elements of grammar, I have included some concise, sharp units on grammar that are focused and should feel pleasurable not onerous to your students.

This is the first year you might want to consider a formal unit on techno-literacy. Technology is new terrain for teachers, but certainly not new for our students. Technology requires different skills in reading and is therefore a key unit in grades 3 through 5. Everything—from what key words to put into a Google search, to browsing and skimming on a Web page—requires reading and writing skills and strategies that are somewhat different from those we use for traditional text.

A reading unit can precede or parallel a writing unit in techno-literacy. Writing skills on the Internet are mainly about how to communicate quickly, effectively, and clearly. In the reading section, there should be critical analysis, as the Internet offers us a written universe that can pour forth from our

Nick DeMillo

computers with very little screening. On the writing side, new protocols for e-mail are evolving all the time. Even salutations for e-mail are in an evolutionary state. It is an exciting time, with an explosion of literacy on the contemporary scene. These units can be an opportunity for you as a teacher to learn alongside your students, researching the Internet to find out what bloggers and the Web experts are saying about e-mail etiquette and what you yourselves think about it. Students can be on the lookout for anchor texts that are exemplar e-mails that come right from their own lives, or fun Web sites they or their parents or friends browse on. E-mail is an incredible tool for connecting us and for connecting ideas across continents. If we want to raise our children to be global citizens, it is imperative that we explicitly teach them how to use such a valuable tool wisely and well.

It is likely your students are just beginning to make significant use of their e-mail relationships with their friends at home, and to use the Internet for basic research for their nonfiction projects under close supervision. Late spring is an excellent time of year to introduce such a unit. You can talk to your students about what it means to be a reader of the Internet, not only in terms of how cautious one must be, but also in terms of the vast array of information that can be found there.

In addition, your third-grade readers are still easily overwhelmed by large quantities of text. When faced with a Web site that seems particularly dense, you can use this opportunity to teach them useful skills and strategies for perusing a screenful of densely worded text. Or, conversely, how to simply move on and find another site that is better suited for their age group.

This year, your students are much more aware of the look of language and the meanings of words. Units you design this year in grammar may involve collecting words of interest, making a wall of wonderful words, and searching for original meanings and sources from other languages for words of interest.

Third graders are ready for deeper investigations into nonfiction, so you may want to support their learning by staggering units such as the ones on note-taking to help them break the parts of becoming a nonfiction reader and writer into manageable pieces. They are ready to handle a lot more, but some of them may still be going home and playing dress-up with their friends. The sample years you see here are designed to keep that lightness and the sociability of a third grader, while providing lots of support for the next steps into a more complex world of language and print.

Grade 4 Calendar — Sample One

PROCESS=red   GENRE=green   STRATEGY=orange   CONVENTIONS=blue

MONTH	READING UNITS	WRITING UNITS
Sept.	The ARCH: Readers Think Across Books	The ARCH: Writers Are Influenced by Literature
Oct.	Sentence Study 1 week	Sentence Study 2 weeks
	Exploring Thinking Through Partnerships 3 weeks	Developing Writing Ideas 2 weeks
Nov.	Making Inferences Across Genres	Narrative
Dec.	The Test as a Genre	Writing to the Prompt
Jan.	Stamina 3 weeks	Stamina 3 weeks
	Pausing Punctuation 1 week	Pausing Punctuation 1 week
Feb.	Mystery Clubs	Writing Fiction
March	Grammar Exploration 2 weeks	Grammar Exploration 2 weeks
	Nonfiction 2 weeks	Nonfiction 2 weeks
April	Nonfiction	Persuasive Articles
May	Theme in Poetry	Rereading Writing to Revise and to Inspire New Ideas 1 week
		Poetry 3 weeks
June	Looking Back, Looking Ahead: Summer Reading Plans	Looking Back, Looking Ahead: Summer Writing Plans

Grade 4 Calendar—Sample Two

PROCESS=red   GENRE=green   STRATEGY=orange   CONVENTIONS=blue

MONTH	READING UNITS	WRITING UNITS
Sept.	The ARCH: Readers Think Across Books	The ARCH: Writers Are Influenced by Literature
Oct.	Fluency 2 weeks	Sentence Variety 2 weeks
	Searching for Theme in Realistic Fiction 2 weeks	The Beginning Essayist: Crafting Paragraphs with Thesis Statements and Text Evidence 2 weeks
Nov.	Realistic Fiction Partnerships	The Beginning Essayist
Dec.	Magazine Study: Strategies for Reading Multiple Texts in Multiple Genres	The Four Prompts
Jan.	Techno-literacy 1 week	Magazine Writing: Informational Article
	Nonfiction 3 weeks	
Feb.	Grammar: Verb Tenses 1 week	Informational Articles 1 week
	Mystery 3 weeks	Writing About Reading: Developing Theories and Supporting Them With Evidence 3 weeks
March	Stamina and Independence	Stamina and Independence
April	Author Clubs 2 weeks	Close Look at an Anchor Text 2 weeks
	Dialogue 2 weeks	Dialogue 2 weeks
May	Making Inferences 1 week	Artful Uses of Punctuation 1 week
	Poetry 3 weeks	Poetry Clubs 3 weeks
June	Looking Back, Looking Ahead: Summer Reading Plans	Looking Back, Looking Ahead: Summer Writing Plans

Teaching/Learning Explanation: Grade 4

The focus of the ARCH this year becomes immediately angled toward thinking across texts and using texts to inspire writing. The students will be very comfortable in a reading and writing environment by the time they reach fourth grade, and can launch into thinking about text connections quickly.

In their writing, students are exploring their own responses to reading explorations, with an early eye toward how they can craft their responses into the shape of an essay. This early sharing in the year is a great way for students to introduce themselves to each other, saying, "This is who I am as a writer. This is who I am as a reader. I use my passions and curiosities to drive my book choice and to guide what will become my thesis statements."

Collaboration remains as essential as ever in the fourth grade, maybe even more important. While students are exponentially more independent in their reading and writing, and at home may be curling up with a book far away from adults, in school we want to keep them closely connected to the talk inspired by literature and the talk inspired by curiosity and inquiry. Fourth graders are deeply social. So much of what they are thinking about all day now concerns their friendships and the ever-changing flows of social interaction in the classroom, after school, on the playground, and at lunch. I have built these years around the idea that I want to capitalize on that fourth-grade preoccupation, offering them lots of opportunity for scaffolded collaboration: beginning with partnerships and moving to fluid clubs, with each new club or partnership giving them a new chance to meet and talk with different people in their classroom.

Fourth graders are able to do a lot. They also feel more independent, so I have built independence into the yearlong plan as something for us to talk about with our students and continue to reinforce. They are savoring the depth of their knowledge about conventions, and any knowledge we can give them about grammar and punctuation may be what they remember for the rest of their lives.

Grade 5 Calendar—Sample One

PROCESS=red   GENRE=green   STRATEGY=orange   CONVENTIONS=blue

MONTH	READING UNITS	WRITING UNITS
Sept.	The ARCH: Readers Consider How Words Change the World	The ARCH: Writers Consider How Their Words Change the World
Oct.	Becoming Readers of Style Guides and Other Resources 1 week	Using Style Guides to Try New Techniques 1 week
	Studying Authors of Short Stories 3 weeks	The Personal Essay 3 weeks
Nov.	Fantasy and Science Fiction	Paragraphing 1 week
		The Short Story 3 weeks
Dec.	Reading Content Area Textbooks 2 weeks	Outlining 2 weeks
	Test Genre 2 weeks	Creating Study Guides 2 weeks
Jan.	Social Action Reading Clubs	Writing About Reading: Supporting the Big Idea With Text Evidence
Feb.	Readers Follow Passions and Explore Ideas Strategically 2 weeks	Persuasive Writing: Essays, Speeches, Letters, and Editorials 3 weeks
	Techno-literacy: Researching Our Topics Online 2 weeks	Editing Techniques 1 week
March	Oral Fluency: Reading One's Writing With Conviction 3 weeks	Revision: Revising for Mood, Tone, and Intention 2 weeks
	Fluency and Punctuation 1 week	Techno-literacy: E-mails and Blogs 2 weeks
April	Poetry Interpretation: Poets Who Change the World	Writing Poetry to Change the World
May	Looking Back: The Books That Changed Our Lives	Reflective Essay 3 weeks
		Paragraphing 1 week
June	Looking Ahead: Middle School Reading Plans	Looking Ahead: Middle School Writing Plans

Grade 5 Calendar—Sample Two

PROCESS=red   GENRE=green   STRATEGY=orange   CONVENTIONS=blue

MONTH	READING UNITS	WRITING UNITS
Sept.	The ARCH: Readers Consider How Words Change the World	The ARCH: Writers Consider How Their Words Change the World
Oct.	Critical Literacy: Content Area Reading Strategies 3 weeks	Writing for the Test: Crafting Document-Based Essays 3 weeks
	Sentence Structure: Naming Types of Sentences 1 week	Sentence Variety 1 week
Nov.	Short-Story Clubs	Writing About Reading: Building and Defending Theories
Dec.	Interpretation Through Poetry and Short Story 2 weeks	Literary Essay 2 weeks
	Reading the Test 2 weeks	Writing to Literary Prompts 2 weeks
Jan.	Author Study	Using Mentor Texts
Feb.	Genre-Based Book Clubs	Fiction-Writing Clubs
March	Reading the Media: Learning to Navigate Newspapers, Internet 3 weeks	Editorials 3 weeks
	The Semicolon 1 week	The Semicolon 1 week
April	Nonfiction: Using Text Sets to Build Background Knowledge	Independent Research Projects
May	Grammar Review 1 week	Grammar Review 1 week
	Historical Fiction 3 weeks	Historical Fiction 3 weeks
June	Looking Back: What Books Changed Your Life This Year?	Looking Back: How Did Your Writing Effect Change this Year?

Teaching/Learning Explanation: Grade 5

In fifth grade, collaboration, readers' responses, and conventional language all continue to be threads we pull to create the consistency of our curriculum. Fifth graders are thinking deeply about the outside world. They are interested in all that goes on around them and outside of them. They are more able to talk about current events at the dinner table with their families, and world events take on new significance and immediacy in their lives. What before felt like the distant world now feels more like their world.

Now even the reading and writing role models they are going to study in the first month of school may not be people they know from their local community or school but might be leaders such as Abraham Lincoln, who valued words and used them to shape the direction of a nation. Or the poet Robert Frost, who led a deceptively simple life as a gentleman farmer, but whose poems conveyed a universal understanding of the human condition.

I reserve specific time for reading/writing units with social justice angles. Text clubs focused on social justice may utilize multiple readings so that the club might read both *Maniac Magee* and a recent article in the newspaper about poverty and teenagers in urban environments. Similarly, your more struggling text club may read *Just Juice* by Karen Hesse, paired with an article about the high rate of illiteracy in our country. Students will use these text connections to inform their rich conversations around these subjects, using primary and secondary resources to support their talk.

In the paired writing experience, students will craft group responses, or individual responses, depending on your preference, to the talk they had in their text clubs and the reading they did, to create plausible final drafts that could truly have an impact on the world. The clubs studying *Maniac Magee* and the theme of poverty and teens might draft a petition to the president asking for more after-school youth-center funding as a means to provide help for these young people. Or these students might consider writing a letter to the writer Dave Eggers, who runs a program for adolescents in California, and perhaps send a small donation to help keep his project going.

The Karen Hesse *Just Juice* club might write a letter to the school newspaper, asking the school to rally around the idea of collecting books for the local residential school for foster care kids. My intent in these units is for my students to see that reading and writing equal action.

Achieving Balance in the Teaching of Reading and Writing

The integration of the teaching of reading and writing means that, at times, one is going to feel larger than the other in your teaching. Over the course of the year, you will generally want to balance your reading and writing instruction. However, you will not necessarily want to equally balance the two every day, or even every week. For example, if you are studying fluency in reading, this unit might last two weeks. You are helping your students read more smoothly, use (respond to/react to) punctuation more effectively, use white space to understand where to pause, and read with good intonation. You then may want to parallel a fluency unit in writing instruction, helping students read their own writing with the same genuine intonation, paying close attention to punctuation and white space, and revising accordingly. This may be a briefer set of lessons than your reading work, perhaps a set of three or four lessons that follows or parallels the reading work you are doing. But the greater portion of the work you are going to do in literacy this month will be in reading.

Sebrenna. Lives at a Beach house With Peppy. Peppy Loves the Bech house. loves The Bech house

This primary writer is studying fiction as a major and print conventions as a minor. Her anchor text is *Knuffle Bunny* by Mo Willem.

Puppy Won and SeBrena Smield at Puppy. SeBrena Sade Hray and that was her ferst werd.

Similarly, in a theme study, you may want to use the read-aloud to model deep talk about theme, while during Independent Practice, students use their own texts at their own levels to explore theme. The culmination of this unit is an essay relating these discoveries. Your work in writing is more compact, as you have done a lot of work both in reading and through talk exercises, which build a student's capacity to write well about the subject. The writing portion of this unit should be clear, goal driven, and focused on the outcome of an essay. Having the opportunity to study theme through reading instruction becomes a sustained opportunity for rehearsal of one's own ideas, culminating in a shorter study involving putting them on paper.

Units should interrelate: they should "talk" to one another. For example, one group of teachers created a yearlong calendar in which the reading unit is Reading in the Content Areas (3 weeks), and the writing unit is Informational/Persuasive Essay (2 weeks). The reading unit is then going to set up the writing unit. For the first two weeks, the entire literacy block will be mostly absorbed by the teaching of reading. Students will be reading;

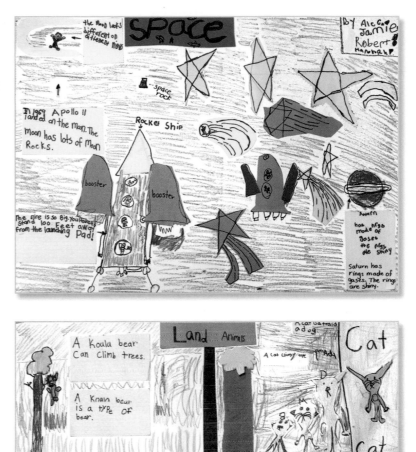

These primary writers are working collaboratively. They are studying nonfiction as a major and partnerships as a minor.

browsing through books; looking at different examples of text books and other materials; reading through primary source material; talking with partners about what they are noticing and finding in their reading; taking notes in their notebooks about their findings and what they are noticing about themselves as readers of content area nonfiction; and using T-charts with the header "What I Am Reading About" on the left-hand side of the page and the header "What I Am Noticing About Myself as a Reader" on the right-hand side of the page.

Beginning in the second week, the students may also begin collecting ideas in their notebooks for an informational essay topic that will be the culmination of the unit. In the third week of the unit, your writing teaching comes more to the fore. You will help the students build understanding and skills necessary for reading content area nonfiction, such as using text features, asking active questions as they read, comparing more than one text as they read, and taking notes on texts. The students may then turn more of their attention to the writing component of this joint study, using what they know as readers to glean more information from the text as writers. As they segue into the writing unit, they come armed with information as to how readers read in the content areas, so as they develop their thesis idea for their essay, they now read more effectively.

This primary writer is studying exploring writing ideas as a major and craft strategies as a minor.

In the writing portion of this unit, the teacher turns her attention to the organization of ideas, showing her students exemplars in which authors have used content area materials to bolster their argument. Students will then spend the bulk of their time writing; reading becomes secondary and supportive to the writing process as students collect ideas, draft, revise, and complete the essay.

In his book *Ox-Cart Man*, Donald Hall writes of the farmer who counts potatoes dug from the brown field, and packs wool sheared in April, all the work he has done all year to take to the market, where he will sell the potatoes and the wool. When the cart is empty, he will sell the cart. When the cart is sold, he will sell the ox and walk home, so the year can begin again. By fire's light in November, he stitches a new harness for next year's ox in the barn, and carves the yoke and builds the cart all over again.

In our teaching, it sometimes feels this way for us. We start our second-grade year over again. There is beauty in this for us. But for our students, it is much, much different. They are not starting their year over; they are moving on a forward line.

This upper grade writer is writing about her reading. Her major is story elements and her minor is writing about reading.

The best of our teaching is to pay attention to both the circle and the forward line. Our best teaching, our children's best learning, is rooted in the circular nature of what we come back to again and again, but there are also the excitement and challenges of a fresh start.

CHAPTER 5

A Unit in the Teaching of Reading and Writing

A unit of study in reading and writing is sustained inquiry that allows for regular practice and requires students to actively commit to their learning. A unit has a clearly identified beginning, middle, and end. Each unit has an instructional focus. A unit on friendship, for example, is too broad unless there is a clear and specific outcome and your students know exactly what it is they are going to study and practice together. A focused renaming of a unit on friendship might be "Inferring Character Relationships" for your more sophisticated readers, or "Identifying Character Traits" for your less sophisticated readers. A theme may be present in a unit if it is important to you and you believe it will inspire your students, but it must be deeply and clearly linked to skills and strategies. Reading and writing units are focused periods of instruction from one to six weeks in length, with the focus from The Complete 4 categories of process, genre, strategy, or conventions. All the lessons in the unit lead up to several key understandings, and lessons will repeat or build upon those taught previously. Each lesson will connect to another and lead to a common goal, and all lessons provide time for exploration, practice, conversation, and reflection.

Initially students are immersed in the topic. During this time the teacher models her thinking, using anchor texts as support; then students and teacher begin to identify and name the attributes of the study topic. Subsequent teaching includes guided practice where students search for these attributes in their own reading, demonstrating increasing independence. Finally, students are asked to commit to their understanding and to continue to draw on these understandings throughout the year. A unit of study offers time for community work and Independent Practice. Both teachers and students have objectives for learning, and the expectation is always that this experience will yield more productive reading and writing behaviors. Although objectives for teaching inside The Complete 4 categories remain constant, individual teachers and students are urged to create the specifics of a unit.

Begin to build your unit by aligning goals and objectives with your standards, setting a framing question, gathering materials to influence/support your unit, and determining what your assessments will be. Be clear about which Complete 4 category this is and select a minor strand from another Complete 4 category; look for examples of your study topic in the world; determine the length of your unit (and adhere to it).

Setting the Framing Question

Your framing question should meet the following criteria:

- Represents worthwhile discussion and study

- Promotes higher-order thinking

- Is complex enough to be broken down into smaller questions

- Is anchored in the lives of learners

- Is relevant to real-world problems

- Is meaningful and interesting to students

- Is open ended and without a simple answer

- Is explicitly connected to your assessment plan for the unit

A framing question for a primary-grade unit on retelling (a strategy unit) might be, "How do recognizing and using story elements help us present an effective retelling?" A fourth-grade unit of study on historical fiction (a genre unit) might have as its framing question, "How does historical fiction help us think about history from a human perspective?" A process study in third grade on book clubs might have as its framing question, "What conversational moves can help us deepen our book talks?" In a fifth-grade conventions unit on commas, the framing question might be, "How can our developing use of the comma extend our writing into more complex sentences and connect two or more big ideas in our thinking?"

Aligning to Standards

The angle you take in building your unit is going to depend on what your standards say, what your expectations for your population of students are, and what you truly love to study with your students. For example, although we may study fiction every year with our students, the unit you develop in second grade is going to look different from the units you develop in third, fourth, and fifth grade for the same genre. Taking the New York state standards as an example, in second grade, there is a focus on characters, whereas in third grade, students must make connections to text, not only with characters but also with setting and plot. In second grade, students are asked to make inferences and predictions through characters. In third grade, they need to do so for events as well. Therefore, a series study using Horrible Harry or another anchor series with strong characters serving as a model is a good angle for second-grade students. Students can reflect standards-based teaching and learning by relating characters in literature to their own lives, and making predictions and drawing inferences as well. In third grade, you may want to angle your fiction study as a retelling study, since the standards ask third graders to relate the setting and the plot to their own lives. There is a larger emphasis on summarizing main ideas and supporting details from imaginative text. In the New York standards in third grade, there is an emphasis on comparative literature. A choice for a fiction study might be called "Comparing Literature Through an Author Study," using master picture-book authors such as Eve Bunting and Patricia Polacco, who write at a sophisticated level with more complicated themes. In fourth grade, students are asked to use knowledge of story structure, elements, and key vocabulary to interpret stories. This might lead you to develop a fiction unit called Reading With a Critical Lens, Searching for Theme in Literature as the major. The minor could be inference.

A theme unit in courage could focus on finding the big idea in one's reading, noting how characters change over time, reading across authors and texts, with a minor strand focusing on how we read books in a series, looking closely at the Narnia series and Harry Potter. Another theme could be explorers, and the unit focus could be reading primary source material, journal writing, simulated journals, and research skills. Yet another theme could be holidays, and the unit focus could be reading in multiple genres, rhyming poems, making inferences, and connecting one's prior experience to text.

Reading and writing units can be integrally connected to content area work. This enables you to build your reading and writing units with an eye toward your content work. If you are doing a colonial history unit in social studies, in March, for example, then in February you might consider making primary source research the main focus of your writing workshop. Or, as you are building a unit called The Qualities of a Good Essay, and you know it will be followed by a social studies unit on the Civil Rights movement, then be sure to angle some of your teaching in your writing unit toward the kind of writing your students will be doing in their social studies unit. Your lessons should build on each other across the content areas. It is very helpful in your nonfiction unit in reading and writing to allow your students some open inquiry if later in the year you are going to do content area research.

If you begin by teaching students how to do research on topics they are interested in and passionate about, later they will be very familiar with the structures and procedures of research when they are engaging in a predetermined group topic. In this way, they have seen the intrinsic value of research. As you are building your reading and writing units, be sure to angle your teaching so that your students understand that later on in their content area work they will be doing similar types of work.

Outcomes and Projects

Each unit of study should have a specific outcome, a public representation of the learning each individual student and the community have done in the unit period's chunk of time. In a genre study, outcomes will be writing projects within that genre. In a six-week upper-grade narrative unit, there should be at least two writing projects completed by the end of the unit, one at the end of the first three weeks, and the other at the end of the second three weeks. In a four-week primary narrative unit, there should be two writing projects. Students may write a simple story based on their new learning about character and plot in the first two weeks. This product is celebrated, shared with parents, and perhaps displayed somewhere in the classroom. The second project adds the new learning of the next two weeks, perhaps some knowledge of setting, and a deepening of the students' understanding of the power of good storytelling. This piece is again celebrated publicly, with further emphasis placed on reflecting on the concrete aspects of each of these story elements that the students learned about in previous weeks.

In a process unit, the writing products for each student may be in different genres and might look quite different. In a study focused on building stamina, Sarah might be reading fiction and writing a book review in response to a great book she has read, while Joe writes a series of three poems in response to the poetry collections he has been perusing. The products will also be written or oral reflections by students on their learning during this study, as well as a completed anchor chart describing what the community learning has been. Sarah, for example, notices she is now reading a certain number of words per minute, an improvement over her previous rate. The book review product is a supplement to the stamina strand, reinforcing it so that the teacher knows that Sarah is not just pushing herself mindlessly through text—that while she keeps up her pace and speed, she also comprehends. Joe is interested in sustaining an idea across three different poems. He is less interested in how fast he can read, because he knows he is a fast reader. He is more interested in his stamina across time in sustaining ideas and developing themes.

For the primary student, the products will also look quite different from student to student. Jenna notices that she now can read three Level C books in one Independent Practice time. She will record this observation on a sticky note so that again, like Sarah's teacher, she can keep track of her comprehension level even as she tries to push herself through books. Ben notices that he is able to have really good text talk with his partner for a sustained period of time. The teacher records student achievement and progress on anchor charts to solidify the learning.

For strategy units, you may want to develop a rubric to help keep you and your students on track and reach outcomes that are clear. For example, in a primary classroom, when students are studying inference, their rubric for fiction might include identifying characters' feelings through illustrations, actions, and words; identifying character traits through actions and words; and finding a "hidden" message through thinking about what a character has learned as well as what the author might want them to learn.

In the upper grades, a rubric for inferring could include such reading behaviors as looking for hidden meanings in metaphors and similes, identifying ways in which characters are changing over time, and finding clues that help us better understand characters and their actions in making strong predictions. Outcomes and products in strategy units can include written responses to reading, completed rubrics, and anchor charts.

Outcomes and products in convention studies should be frequent and public. For example, if you are doing a sentence study with an upper-grade class, and the study lasts two weeks, every third day, students should "publish" a well-constructed sentence based on the learning you have been doing together about building effective sentences. A final outcome might also be a rubric about what a powerful sentence comprises and a way for students to look at their own writing and self-assess. The final products in a conventions unit might be a paragraph with five or six well-constructed sentences interplaying with one another. Your assessment in this unit of your students' progress will be in part based on this final project.

In a primary classroom, the outcomes and products in a two-week conventions unit could also be a simple rubric asking students to make note of where they have correctly used ending punctuation and space between words. Anchor charts that define uses for punctuation and sentence structure are also helpful here so students can refer to them as the year unfolds. At regular intervals throughout the study (e.g., every third day), you can ask your students to put a star next to a sentence they really like in the work they have done, and copy those onto sentence strips to hang up in the classroom. In both primary and upper-grade classrooms, having students notice and copy great writing from texts they admire and hang them up with an eye toward pointing out what is working in that sentence is another outcome/product for studies in conventions.

Assessment

Each year and each unit should have ongoing opportunities for both informal assessment and more formal assessment points, both at the beginning and end of each unit. This record keeping will be immensely helpful to you. Informal assessment opportunities include the following:

> **Conferring.** Your individual focused discussions with students that are guided by your lessons, your unit focus, and your knowledge of each child. You should enter a conference with a strong sense of who this child is as a reader and writer and what you want him or her to accomplish today. But the beauty of a conference is your openness to that incredible moment when the child shares something in the midst of her work that feels revelatory

and helps you better understand her process so you can guide her toward the next steps.

Whole-class observations. Take at least three minutes (allow yourself!) to stop during Independent Practice and observe the room: What is the energy there? How are your children working together? Alone? What are you noticing?

The Wrap-Up information. Allow a few minutes during the Wrap-Up for children to ask questions about the day's work or the work of the unit. If they expect this, they will respond to the structure and bring questions or confusions to the larger group.

Formal assessments include the following:

Unit-designed assessments. Please see the unit samples beginning on page 150 for examples of easy-to-use assessment tools. These are adaptable to the needs of your particular school community.

The state tests. Use the results to guide your practice, not overwhelm it! There is plenty of valuable information to be found if you gain access to the results and can do statistical analyses, which will give you important information about students. For example, in one school, the principal discovered that girls were performing more poorly on questions referring to nonfiction text. The school spent many faculty meetings talking about how to help girls find their voices and comfort levels in the reading of nonfiction and how to ensure that during independent reading, girls were encouraged to read more nonfiction. Even these small observations can lead to major revisions in teaching practice and overall goal setting.

What Degree of Choice Will Students Have During a Unit of Study?

There should certainly be some measure of choice in the guided practice component of our unit of study. But our students blossom under different circumstances, and they might need a great deal of scaffolding in order to make wise choices. For example, in a poetry study, I may want my entire class to take a close look at Robert Frost, but during the guided practice portion of the unit, I would allow my students to select which Frost poem will become their anchor text. This holds true for a series study as well. You might use Nate the Great as your anchor series. All your students are reading that series together with you, but students could talk about characters who appeal to them and compare notes.

In other units, choice becomes far broader; it is part of the work we are doing to build independence in our students. For example, if your unit is about writing clubs that help students collaborate and talk well about their writing, the choice of what to write or what genre they will be writing in becomes part of the writer's decision making as well as part of your assessment of this writer. If you develop a unit on setting goals as readers, individual students will be offered far more choice because you are focusing more on student process rather than group product. This unit may be just two weeks long, and the outcome may be that you want your students to work on one or two specific reading goals that they set for themselves. Each set of goals will be and should be very different for each child in the class.

Welcome to the Stages of a Unit

Like a really good poem, content looks and feels a lot richer when it is supported by a sturdy structure. It is helpful to think about the four stages of a unit of study as you plan and create units of your own or follow along with mine. These stages of a unit can be applied to every Complete 4 category.

Stage 1: Immersion

The purpose of immersion is to surround students with the sounds of a genre, the habits of mind of good readers and writers, the qualities of great writing, and the powerful strategy work that effective readers and writers use to delve into text. In Stage 1, students will record and share their noticings of a process, genre, strategy, or convention. If I am going to study nonfiction expert books with my students, I am going to collect Jim Arnosky books such as *All About Owls* and *All About Sharks*. In Stage 1, students will partner together to read and enjoy them. The teacher will read them aloud. Students and teachers will notice the way the books are written, and read others in the same genre. Students will begin to compare and contrast these texts. How are they the same? What does reading across texts tell us about this genre? You will ask them to notice text features and graphic aids that are indicators of this genre.

In a process unit on text talk, in Stage 1 students may demonstrate their informal conversations about short shared texts. The teacher might even show a short video of excellent text talk, and ask students to comment on what they notice about the talk and what makes it good.

In a strategy unit, students may bring books they have previously read in their Independent Practice to the conversation, discussing themes they have noticed. The teacher might chart how the themes are found, and what the students noticed about theme and text in prior reading experiences. The teacher might also make connections to other aspects of the students' lives, through the lens of theme—asking students to find theme in movies and songs—and even through interactions and experiences with family and friends, that appear to be united by common threads.

In a conventions unit, students may bring to the lesson their own writing or writing they really admire, noticing elegant uses of ellipses, or artful, meaning-altering uses of the parentheses.

Stage 2: Identification

The poet W. S. Auden once said that the ultimate test for a poet is the proper naming of a cat. The ability to name things is at the heart of learning and understanding, enabling us to define and convey what we see and experience. As we study a genre, we identify the major qualities of that genre, and over time, as the grades spiral upward, we name more and more subtle qualities of the genre. Studying process, we identify the major qualities of success for that process. Studying a strategy, we identify what we mean by that strategy and how we use it. Studying conventions, we name each convention and its many uses. Our thinking is recorded in public ways: anchor charts, readers' and writers' notebooks, the teacher's own notebook, SMART Boards, and blogs. Your teaching role is to name the attributes/elements of the study and define them, both alongside your students and a bit ahead of them, so that as they discover, you name, and as they name, you record. In Stage 2, don't be afraid to provide attributes and definitions of the qualities of whatever it is you are studying. This is your opportunity to teach very assertively. In a nonfiction unit, for example, at this point you would name the type of structure of the book, identify the purpose of the book, categorize it as persuasive or informational nonfiction, and identify text features and graphic aids. In writing nonfiction, you are identifying and naming topics of interest to you and showing how they fit into the category of nonfiction. In a process unit on text talk, at Stage 2 you will name the attributes of powerful text talk. For younger readers, this might have more to do with the children learning how to sit with a partner knee to knee, one of the behaviors that lead us to good talk. For older readers, the identification may be to name conversational moves such as teaching students to add on to what others say, and charting that as a really good way to go deeper into text talk. In a strategy unit on theme study, you will identify a working definition of theme. It might be one you come up with as a class, or it might be one that you present to your students at this time to help them move further through the study. In the identification phase of a conventions unit, this would be a good opportunity to introduce standard definitions of punctuation usage from different grammatical sources, depending on the ages of your children, and also to create a class definition of each of the punctuation elements you are studying, which you can chart and feature in the classroom.

Stage 3: Guided Practice

This is the heart of the study. If the study is short, the guided practice may last just two days. If the study is longer, it may be two weeks. Using anchor texts, transcripts, think-alouds, role plays, read-alouds, write-alouds, student anecdotes, and video, you will model exemplary attributes or behaviors with the students actively participating through their Independent Practice. Your students will practice teacher-led and sometimes student-generated exercises that will lead to increased independence. In a genre study on nonfiction, students have selected their topic of research and chosen their resources. They evaluate the resources for whether they will answer the questions they have set out to investigate. In a third-grade classroom, the students will categorize their facts, then use their resource to find missing information as they read. During writing time, they are collecting, drafting, crafting topic sentences that hold facts, and asking themselves which of the facts they have read about will support their big idea.

For example, a student finds out that a musk ox has horns and long, thin fur, and that it bellows. During guided practice, the teacher encourages students to organize their facts, asking, "What do these facts have in common?" A student discovers through this reading that a musk ox can defend himself in many different ways. This becomes his topic sentence during writing time, and the facts he has read about become examples that support this topic sentence. Younger students will make a picture plan, and all students will be using mentor texts. In a nonfiction unit, students may model their work on Jim Arnosky's writing, borrowing his structures, graphic aids, and features, in order to create their own books.

In guided practice during a process study on text talk, students will use shared texts to build conversations across a two- to three-day period. They will be taking note of their conversational moves, such as *how we made our conversation go deeper* and *what helped us take a turn in our conversation*. They will be paying special attention to quiet and loud voices in the group and to their efforts as a community to encourage the quieter voices, and they will be charting this, too. They will study transcripts of each other's talk, highlighting what works well and what does not. The teacher will continue to model whole-class talk through the read-aloud. In a strategy study on theme, during guided practice, students will dig into their own independent reading to uncover themes related to the community conversation. If our read-aloud contains a strong thread on social justice or world peace, then students will search for examples in their own reading for theme connections. Students will use notebooks or writing folders to track their own reactions as they read, and evidence of theme in their own texts. This unit may include a culminating essay in response to reading with a focus on theme. The guided practice period allows students to work on their theme essays with close supervision by the teacher.

In a conventions study, in the guided practice portion, students will read their independent texts with an eye toward how their authors are using commas, look for examples of punctuation in their own independent reading, and keep a notebook to record elegant sentences they find in their own reading. The guided practice will also include opportunities for students to practice crafting elegant sentences of their own, inspired by the books they are reading. Students will be expected to make a case for how their use of conventions is adding to the meaning of their sentence construction.

Stage 4: Commitment

From the start of the study, you have been looking for and sharing examples of student work/behaviors that you expect to become more and more integrated into the ongoing work of your community. At the crucial juncture of the commitment stage, the work you have been doing shifts becoming inextricably linked to the work you are about to do in the next unit. The commitment stage records what you and your students have learned in this unit, assessing each student individually, as well as assessing your community's growth. How is what we have learned in this unit going to inform our thinking as we begin the next? It is essential that you include your students in this transitional thinking. Lead your students through some reflection and self-assessment, while at the same time you assess their work and progress and establish expectations for future work. Your students will integrate behaviors/strategies relevant to this unit into their independent reading and writing lives and will understand that they will be held accountable according to their capacities for carrying this work forward and applying it to the next unit. They will be expected to show evidence of this learning through their writing, reading talk, actions, and expectations.

In the commitment phase in a nonfiction unit, the students are charting what they have learned as note-takers and about the research process that they can use in future writing. They may discuss tips on how to take notes without plagiarizing. In a process study on text talk, students may record in their notebooks a top-ten list of great conversational moves that propel a conversation forward and help it take new turns when an idea seems dead. In a theme study, students will identify strategies for uncovering a theme in text, such as making inferences, discussing traits of main characters, and creating plot maps that show connections across pages. These theme strategies will help students uncover big ideas even as they read in other genres. In a conventions study, students will make a final learning chart (an anchor chart) that sums up

concrete and helpful new understandings about some elements of punctuation. In one class, for example, a student commented that a semicolon is like a wedding ring, permanently connecting two key ideas. This kind of observation would be recorded on an anchor chart. Students would be expected and encouraged to use the semicolon efficiently, effectively, and artfully in future units.

The Commitment	The Carry-over Into New Learning
Metaphor and poetry	Metaphor and narrative
Questioning the text in a nonfiction unit	Questioning big ideas and talk in a text talk unit
Extended use of the comma in a punctuation study	Extended use of the comma in a completed essay in an essay unit
Identifying key ideas and evidence from text in a note-taking unit	Making use of key ideas and evidence from text in a nonfiction unit
Recognizing structures in a nonfiction unit	In a content area research unit, applying a specific structure of nonfiction text to one's own writing ideas

Now that we have journeyed through the stages of a unit, let me show you examples of a units in each Complete 4 category so you can see it in its entirety. To help you get your bearings, I have included here some helpful language you may use with your students during Focused Instruction to guide you through a unit.

Here is a sample unit in The Complete 4 category of process.

Stage of the Study	Anchor Language
Immersion	Discover, notice, explore, investigate, reflect
Identification	Name, Identify, select, determine
Guided Practice	Try, find, practice
Commitment	Celebrate, reflect, assess, commit, connect

Unit of Study: Stamina
Complete 4 Category: Process

Length of Time: 3 weeks

Grade Level: Upper

Reading Framing Question: How can I help students read longer, stronger, and faster?

Writing Framing Question: How can I help students write longer, stronger, and faster?

Unit Goals
- Students will demonstrably read longer, stronger, and faster.
- Students will be able to identify elements of their process and strategy work that help them do so.
- Students will demonstrably write longer, stronger, and faster.
- Students will be able to identify elements of their process and strategy work that help them to do so.

Anchor Texts
- Students' own writing
- Texts of various lengths and genres, including magazines, comics, poetry, fiction, nonfiction

Note that some days I do not do a Focused Instruction in both reading and writing because there is such a seamless connection between the two. And on other days, I choose to have two separate lessons. With practice, you will be able to sense when you need either one lesson or two, and there is no right answer. But this paralleling helps you maximize your time, and it helps your students understand what your goals are.

Immersion Stage

Day 1

Reading

FI: "Like athletes, readers and writers build muscles to help them become strong. Let's reflect on what athletes do to build endurance." (Build chart together). Possible statements:

- They do things that are healthy for them.
- They discover what will make them stronger and faster: foods, time of day to exercise, etc.

"Notice today what feels good and strong for you as you read."

IP: Students read independently.

WU: Chart noticings.

Writing

IP: "Write independently, choosing your topic and genre. Notice yourself as a writer."

WU: Chart noticings.

Day 2

Reading

FI: "Yesterday we noticed what felt good for us as readers. We noticed text choice and will add that to the chart. When we read something we like, we tend to read longer, stronger, and faster. Today, in making a choice, think carefully about what you will read in terms of those categories. What is going to help you read with the most stamina? Is it a comic, a magazine, a poetry collection, your novel? Is it a text that is slim or thick? With pictures or without? Small font or large? Be honest and make a good choice. Put three choices in your book box."

IP: "Make wise selections and read independently, changing your choices if they are not feeling right."

WU: Students share choices with a partner.

Writing

FI: "Making good topic choices is a way to keep your energy high for writing. How do you know when a topic choice is a good one?"

IP: "Make wise topic choices; switch if one is not working."

WU: Students share choices with a partner.

Day 3

Reading

FI: "Today, in both reading and writing, let's pay close attention to what in our environment helps us read and write longer, stronger, and faster."

IP: Students read independently.

WU: Chart what students notice about environmental supports for their reading (comfort, time, noise levels, etc.).

Writing

IP: "Write independently or with a partner. Notice what works for you or does not work for you in this environment."

WU: "What changes might we make to better support reading and writing longer, stronger, and faster?"

Day 4

Reading

FI: "Whether we are reading or writing, genre itself plays a role in how we feel about our reading and writing. Today, in both reading and writing time, let's try to read and write in a couple of different genres and note how we read/write in each one."

IP: "Read independently but switch genre at least once during the time. Notice how your reading habits or behaviors change, if at all. Think about the effect genre has on your reading."

Writing

IP: "Write independently, switching genre at least once. Notice how your writing habits or behaviors change, if at all. Think about the effect genre has on your writing."

WU: Share together: "How does genre affect your capacity to read longer, stronger, and faster?"

Identification Stage

Day 5

Reading

FI: "The way we name reading and writing in strong, long, and fast ways is called stamina. Building stamina is very important to becoming a lifelong reader and writer. In this unit, we will explore all the reasons we can do those things, and also how we can push ourselves to get even better at them."

IP: "Choose to read and write today during this time, in any way that feels comfortable for you. We will save some of this independent work time for you to meet as partners and discuss your general findings about stamina in your own reading and writing life. Use evidence: When did you find yourself reading and writing longer, stronger, and faster, and why?"

Writing

IP: Same as above.

WU: Identify stamina as:
- reading/writing strong
- reading/writing long
- reading/writing fast

Create a chart to reflect this definition

Guided Practice Stage

Day 6

Reading

FI: "Today we are going to practice reading for a longer period of time than we usually do. Find a way to make this time work for you. You may have to change texts, or genres, or make a shift in your environment." (Show your own examples of what you do to keep your stamina high.)

IP: Students read independently for a longer period of time.

WU: "What worked? What did not? How successful were we today?"

Writing

No writing time today to allow more time for reading.

Day 7

Reading

No reading time today to allow more time for writing.

Writing

FI: "Today we are going to practice writing for a longer period of time. Find a way to make this work for you. You may have to change topics, or genres, or make a shift in your environment." (Show your own examples of what you do to keep your energy high for writing.)

IP: Students write independently.

WU: "What worked? What did not? How successful were we today?"

Day 8

Reading

FI: Model what you do when you get to hard parts in your reading. What print and comprehension strategies do you as a reader use to get you through the hard parts?

IP: Students practice using strategies to get through the hard parts in their reading.

WU: Keep track of these strategies by charting and note-taking.

Writing

FI: Model what you do when you get to the hard parts in your writing. Identify if it is a strategy challenge (i.e., brainstorming ideas) or a conventions challenge (i.e., spelling).

IP: Students practice using strategies to get through the hard parts in their writing.

WU: Keep track of these strategies by charting and note-taking.

Day 9

Reading

FI: "Today we are going to talk about speed. Sometimes the best way to practice speed in reading is to read either a text that is actually a little too easy for you or a text you have already read." Model with a read-aloud you have read before. "Why does rereading help make us faster as readers? Also notice how you 'chunk' your reading more as you read faster."

IP: Students practice reading faster. "Time yourself. Try to 'chunk' your reading. Choose text that is truly comfortable for you, or a text you have read before."

WU: "Which texts helped you read faster and why?"

Writing

FI: "Today let's try writing faster, too. What would help us write faster?" Model what works for you in terms of strategies that help you write faster. Model on a SmartBoard or overhead. Demonstrate thinking down the page as fluently as possible. "Some of this is mental: just get down the page as fast as you can. Some is about setting a goal for yourself."

IP: "Set goals and set your timer and let's see how fast and how much you can write in a specified time."

WU: Students share with a partner.

Day 10

Reading and Writing

FI: "Let's sum up what our findings are so far in both reading and writing. Let's chart what helps us read longer, stronger, and faster."

IP: "In both reading and writing, we use strategies that will help us get down the page efficiently and fluently. Practice these today and use your time for reading and/or writing today."

WU: Have one student model his/her reading/writing stamina strategies.

Day 11

Reading and Writing

FI: "Stamina is also about staying longer with an idea or a topic—an idea or a theme in reading and a topic in writing."

IP: "Choose a text set today that reflects a theme you want to read about over time. Choose a topic you can 'stick with' over time. Read and/or write today in a way that represents stamina in a topic or theme."

WU: "At the end of this unit, we will share a reflection of what is really working for us, as well as a portion of some writing we did in these last three weeks."

Day 12

Reading

FI: Notice what worked well – student anecdotes.

IP: Some students are reading independently, and some are writing independently, some are working on the overhead or SMART Board to practice writing fluently and fast down a page.

WU: Share student work and observations.

Writing

FI: Notice what worked well – student anecdotes.

IP: Students continue working on their writing.

WU: Students share portions of their writing with a partner.

Commitment Stage

Day 13

Reading and Writing

FI: Chart final noticings on what builds stamina in both reading and writing.

IP: "Work on your reflection piece. Include specifics about books you have read and minutes read, as well as topics, genres, and strategies that felt successful (or not)."

WU: Share new strategies or successes.

Day 14

Reading

No reading time today.

Writing

IP: Students work on reflection piece for the final day.

WU: Read strong lines from a few reflections.

Day 15

Reading and Writing

FI: "Share your own reflection on what you have noticed about yourself as a reader/writer developing stamina."

IP: Celebrate and share reflections and evidence as well as brief writing excerpts.

Writing

WU: Affirm the many ways to honor reading and writing, and stress that time, attention to topic and text choice, and speed, all matter in terms of how students grow as readers and writers.

Here, let's take a look at a Complete 4 unit inside the category of conventions. This is a Sentence Study unit.

Unit of Study: Effective Sentence Structures
Complete 4 Category: Conventions

Length of Time: 2 weeks

Grade Level: Upper

Reading Framing Question: How can I help students attend to sentence structure and variety in their reading?

Writing Framing Question: How can I help students expand understanding of sentence structures and build sentence variety into their own writing?

Unit Goals
- Students will identify fragments and run-on sentences and determine uses for each one, where necessary.
- Students will identify fragments and run-on sentences and determine when each one is not to be used in that context, making the necessary corrections.
- Students will use mentor sentences from authors they like, to help them build their own effective sentences.

Anchor Texts
- *Mr. George Baker*, Amy Hest and Jon J. Mulh
- *The Elements of Style, Fourth Edition*, William Strunk, Jr., E. B. White, and Roger Angell

Note that this unit is only two weeks long. One beauty of The Complete 4 system is its attention to variety of unit length. A short but effective unit on an aspect of conventions is a way to highlight for your students the big ideas in your teaching, and also to "punctuate" your year with some intensive learning in these areas.

Immersion Stage

Day 1

Reading

FI: "As I read aloud today" (choose any favorite), "write in your notebook a sentence you really love."

IP: "In your own reading today, keep a written record of sentences that feel particularly effective."

WU: "What do you like about these sentences? Let's name what we like."

Writing

FI: "Revisit your writing notebook to look for sentences you have written that you like."

IP: "Reread your writing and search for examples."

WU: Students share sentences. Make a chart.

Day 2

Reading

FI: Give out a typed text of a favorite picture book or short story. Also show it on an overhead or SmartBoard. "Today you will highlight sentences that you feel are particularly effective."

IP: Students highlight effective sentences.

Writing

FI: "Revisit your writing notebook with a partner to look for and study sentences you like. Together, write new sentences that reflect what you like about the others."

WU: Begin to chart effective sentences (both published and created by students).

Identification Stage

Day 3

Reading

FI: Name parts of a sentence. Use one of the effective sentences selected to name the parts.

IP: "Look for effective sentences in your reading; collect them and name their parts."

WU: "Sentences have predictable components. This is the grammar of a sentence."

Writing

IP: "Write ten effective sentences. Share them with a partner. Name each other's sentence grammar."

WU: Use some student examples to show parts of a sentence.

Day 4

Reading

FI: Identify the difference between a sentence and a fragment and the purposes of each one.

IP: Students look for fragments in their reading.

WU: Students share fragment samples.

Writing

FI: Read aloud *Mr. George Baker*. Note run-ons, intentional and unintentional, as well as fragments. "Why might writers use these as craft techniques?" Chart this.

IP: "Choose a writing topic and write with a purposeful intention to use fragments, run-ons, and conventional sentences."

WU: "Why did you make the decisions you did? What is it about each of these kinds of sentences that helps add to the meaning of the text?"

Day 5

Reading

FI: "A run-on that is not intentional can be corrected through the introduction of periods to separate thoughts, the use of conjunctions and commas to create compound sentences, the use of commas, and the proper use of phrases to create complex sentences."

IP: "Read independently and choose two or more sentences that you like."

WU: "What do you like about these sentences?"

Writing

FI: "Look for examples of run-ons in your own writing that are not intentional. If you find any, correct them with appropriate punctuation."

IP: Students investigate their own writing and correct.

WU: "Where did you make changes?"

Day 6

Reading

FI: Explain the role of a preposition in a complex sentence. Define simple, compound, and complex sentences using examples from your own writing.

IP: Using the text of Mr. George Baker, have students find and name types of sentences: simple, compound and complex.

Writing

IP: "Using your own writing, find and name types of sentences."

WU: Make a chart for all three categories: simple, compound, complex.

Guided Practice Stage

Day 7

Reading

FI: Share exemplars from anchor texts. Build ideas about the effects that sentence length and a variety of sentence lengths and types in a paragraph have on meaning.

Writing

IP: "Write a paragraph of your choosing, using a variety of sentence lengths and types."

WU: Students share with a partner. "What was the effect of sentence length and variety on the meaning of your text?"

Day 8

Reading

FI: Share exemplars from anchor texts.

IP: "Keep an eye on your independent reading to record examples you find."

WU: Students share examples with a partner.

Writing

IP: "Write fragments and run-ons, and share with partners. Build better sentences with an attention to how length affects rhythm and thereby the mood of the work."

WU: Chart sentence samples.

Day 9

Reading

FI: Use an anchor text to model excellent compound sentences and complex sentences.

IP: "In your own independent reading today, be looking for compound and complex sentences that feel effective."

Writing

FI: "Today we are going to revise a passage from our notebook using all we are learning about sentences."

IP: "Rework your sentences with intention. Use variety and be deliberate. Name what you do and also how what you do affects or supports the meaning of the text."

WU: Chart sentence samples and how the structure enhanced meaning.

Commitment Stage

Day 10

Reading

FI: Develop a list of the qualities of an effective sentence.

IP: Students celebrate the revised passage from their notebooks and read them with partners.

Writing

WU: "What have you learned about building effective sentences? Going forward, what will stick with you? We have learned that each sentence has its own architecture, and its length can add meaning to your work. Sentences should vary in length to create a mood and rhythm."

Please take a look at a primary unit of study in genre. The template is the same; the lessons are angled toward the primary reader and writer. Because this is a genre study, the time frame is a bit longer.

Unit of Study: Narrative
Complete 4 Category: Genre

Length of Time: 4 weeks

Grade Level: Primary

Reading Framing Question: How can I help my students recognize story elements in their reading?

Writing Framing Question: How can I help my students implement story elements in their writing?

Unit Goals
- Students will recognize the beginning, middle, and end of a story.
- Students will use these three elements to help plan their own writing.
- Students will recognize story elements of character, setting, plot, and time.
- Students will use story elements to deepen and develop their own writing.

Anchor Texts
- *Knuffle Bunny*, Mo Willem
- *The Mitten*, Jan Brett
- *Tacky the Penguin*, Helen Lester and Lynn M. Munsinger
- *Strega Nona*, Tomie dePaola
- *Sammy the Seal*, Syd Hoff

Other Resources: Planning paper for beginnings, middles, and endings; Tomie dePaola's Web site: www.tomie.com

Immersion Stage

FI: Focused Instruction **IP:** Independent Practice **WU:** Wrap-Up

Day 1

FI: "Today we are going to begin a unit on fiction." Read aloud *Sammy the Seal* by Syd Hoff. "Turn and talk with a partner: What was your favorite part? Was it at the beginning, middle, or end?" Do a three-section chart on beginning, middle, end.

IP: "Read in your book box with an eye to favorites and parts of stories you love and want to share. Visit with a partner to browse in your book boxes. Share favorite texts, pointing out when you liked the beginning, middle, or end."

WU: Share beginnings, middles, or ends that felt exciting, important, or just good in some way.

Day 2

FI: Read aloud *Tacky the Penguin*. Note beginning, middle, and end, with a special attention to the turning point in the text, in the middle. Notice what the purpose for a beginning, middle, and end is.

IP: "Choose one of your independent books. Read it. As you read, be thinking about the middle. Where is there a turning point?"

WU: Chart turning points.

Day 3

FI: Read aloud *Knuffle Bunny*. Chart the beginning, middle, and end. Find the turning point. Name the resolution. "Today, in independent practice, we are going to note these in our own reading."

IP: Students read. "As you read, be thinking about turning points in your texts. Find one you'd really like to share with a partner."

WU: "We are studying the parts of story, especially the moment when something changes, the turning point. What can we say we are noticing about it?" Chart noticings.

Day 4

FI: Read aloud *Knuffle Bunny* again. "What is the kickoff event? That usually comes at the beginning. What is the purpose for it?"

IP: "Reread a favorite from your book box. What do you notice about the beginning and a kickoff event? What is it doing to set up the rest of the story?"

WU: "Tomorrow we will talk about the tie-up, the way a story comes to a close. Tonight, when you read at home, be thinking about the tie-up in your bedtime story."

Day 5

FI: Reread *Sammy the Seal*. Name the qualities that make the ending feel strong. "How do things get tied up in the end?"

IP: "Reread or choose a new text you can read in one sitting, and think deeply about the ending."

WU: "This week we talked about beginnings, middles, and endings. Each one serves a purpose." Anchor chart: the purposes of beginnings, middles, and endings.

Day 6

FI: "Last week we talked about beginnings, middles, and endings. Today I am going to give you paper with a box to represent each part of a story. Take a minute to tell a partner a story with each of the three parts."

IP: Students use their planning page to tell a story with three parts (beginning: set-up; middle: turning point; ending: tie-up).

WU: Share your observations of student writing.

Day 7

FI: "Story ideas can come from people's lives even when the stories are imaginary." Revisit the books read last week to talk about where story ideas come from; even when characters are imaginary, stories feel real. "Problems and solutions are real. Characters feel real in their emotions. Sammy, Tacky, and the girl in *Knuffle Bunny* all feel real. Stories come from our lives but can be imaginary."

IP: "Use this time to write a story, either using your planning page or not, and tell a story that could be imaginary but has real emotion."

WU: "Stories can be imaginary and still feel real."

Day 8

FI: Read aloud *Strega Nona*. "Here we have another story that is imaginary, but it comes from Tomie dePaola's real life." Read information on his family background. "Stories may be imaginary, but they come from real memories. The turning points in stories are often the most imaginary parts of stories."

IP: "Write your own story where you use some of your own memories to create an imaginary story. Think about the turning point as being your most imaginative opportunity."

WU: Students share turning points. Chart turning points.

Identification Stage

Day 9

FI: "The stories we have read all have some things in common. They have elements we find in every story we read. They are character, plot, setting, and time. Let's chart two of the stories we have read so we can confirm they have these elements." Reread *Tacky* or *Sammy*.

Show the students how you can retell one of these stories, noting each of these elements.

IP: "Tell a story you have read to a partner, looking together for examples of the elements."

WU: "What elements did you hear in your partner's story?"

Day 10

FI: "I am going to write my own story in front of you. It's about a magic flying dog. My dog does not fly, but it feels as if she does! Now I am going to retell my story to a partner to see if it has all the elements."

IP: "Tell a new story to your partner before you write anything down. Then write it down."

WU: "How does retelling help you remember your story?"

Guided Practice Stage

Day 11

FI: Read aloud a student piece. Map out its beginning (the setup), the middle (the turning point), and the end (the tie-up). Name the elements: characters, setting, passage of time, and plot. Use a four-square page to name the elements.

IP: Students read and look informally for elements of story in their texts.

WU: "What did you notice?"

Day 12

FI: Read aloud *Knuffle Bunny*. Use a four-square page to map out elements. "Remember that the plot is what we talked about in the first week of our unit, the turning point being the key."

IP: Students read and look for elements in the stories they are reading, and share with a partner.

WU: Chart the elements of a story.

Day 13

FI: "We are going to take a close look at one element of story: character. What are your favorite characters in the stories you read? Why? What are their traits?" (List.) "Characters sometimes stay the same (Nate the Great, Frog and Toad), and sometimes they change."

IP: Students read. "Notice if your characters stay the same or change." Students write. "Try writing about a character who changes. Try writing about a character who will always stay the same" (a series idea).

WU: Chart characters who change and characters who stay the same in stories students read and write.

Day 14

FI: "Let's look at another element of story: setting. What are your favorite settings in the stories you read? Why? What are their characteristics?" (List). "Setting is generally really important to a story" (*Sammy the Seal*: school; *Knuffle Bunny*: city laundromat; *Strega Nona*: small town). List why the settings feel important in each of these stories.

IP: "Find examples of setting in your book as you read. Do you think it's important to the story? In your writing today, try to build up the setting so it matters. Or write a small piece about a place."

WU: Celebrate setting; share lines that help the reader visualize a sense of place.

Commitment Stage

FI: "Look at your book box. Think about what you are learning about story and about fiction, about the telling and making of a story. Take today to browse through your own stories you have been writing and the stories you have been reading. By the end of the week, let us write a new story based on all of our learning. Let's let our thinking carry us forward."

IP: Students write and read. "Today make a story based on your learning."

WU: Share learning. Share lines from new stories.

FI: "Let's revisit the two big ideas we talked about these past weeks: the three big parts of a story, the containers (beginning, middle, end), and then the four elements (character, plot, time, and setting). Time is the trickiest. Let's look at it in our books. *Sammy the Seal* takes place in one day, *Knuffle Bunny* in one hour, *Strega Nona* over several days. As a writer, you get to decide how much time to take in your story."

IP: Students read. "Notice the passing of time in your books." Students write. "Try to use time more deliberately. See what you can do."

WU: Chart ways to use time in stories, applying what students noticed today and what they tried in their writing.

FI: "Today we are going to finish our stories so we can share them tomorrow. Look through them for strong characters, clear setting, the passage of time, and the journey through the story itself, from the setup to the turning point to the tie-up. See if you have all these pieces. Checking in on that is your revision."

IP: Student revise stories.

WU: "What did you add to your piece today?"

FI: "We are going to celebrate our pieces today by reading them to a partner and then by adding a cover and putting them in our classroom library."

IP: Students write and revise; add a cover.

WU: Visit around the room to take a look at the stories.

FI: "We learned so much about stories, from both reading them and writing them. Fiction is how writers make connections between what is real and what is imaginary. No matter what kind of writing you are doing, you can weave both what is real and what is magical into your writing."

IP: Students share ideas for future writing with a partner.

WU: Compliments, final thoughts.

Let's look at one final unit: a primary unit in strategy. Again, the template is the same, and again, we see a lot of synergy between reading and writing. Each Complete 4 category works very well inside this template, and you will find that creating your own units helps you clarify your teaching, use the resources you have, and plan wisely for outcomes.

Unit of Study: Finding the Big Idea/Theme
Complete 4 Category: Strategy

Length of Time: 2 weeks

Grade Level: Primary

Reading Framing Question: How can I help my students recognize that writers develop ideas in the texts they read?

Writing Framing Question: How can I help my students incorporate big ideas in their writing?

Unit Goals
- Students will recognize ideas that have significance in text.
- Students will recognize that every genre offers the opportunity to develop ideas .
- Students will recognize that authors have favorite big ideas they return to again and again.
- Students will be able to identify big ideas in their own writing.
- Students will be able to use strategies for their own writing that will help them find and demonstrate big ideas.

Anchor Text/s
- *Come On, Rain*, Karen Hesse
- *Owen & Mzee: The True Story of a Remarkable Friendship*, Isabella Hatkoff, Craig Hatkoff, and Dr. Paula Kahumbu
- "Poem," Langston Hughes
- *In the Fiddle Is a Song*, Durga Bernhard

Immersion Stage

FI: Focused Instruction **IP:** Independent Practice **WU:** Wrap-Up

Day 1

FI: Preview *Come On Rain*. "What is the sensation you get, and how do you sense the mood from the title and the cover?"

Read aloud. "Jot down a word on your sticky note when you feel an emotion as I read, to remind you of where you felt it. Were your hunches about the sensation, the mood, right? This unit is about the big idea in writing. Sometimes the big idea comes upon us slowly or in a wave; it is a feeling we are experiencing."

IP: "Take some time in your independent reading today to browse, feeling the mood or sensation of each of your books. Select one to share with a partner. Tell your partner what kind of mood there is in this piece."

WU: "Books have moods and sensations. What did you notice in your independent reading today?"

Day 2

FI: Revisit *Come On, Rain*. "We are going to make a list of the big ideas in this text. Big ideas are not always written; they are felt. Let's chart what we think the ideas might be in this story. What is felt?"

IP: Students read independently. "Think about the big ideas in your reading. Place sticky notes where you have a hunch a big idea is indicated."

WU: Students share their sticky-note page with a partner.

Day 3

FI: "How do readers search for the big ideas? Big ideas are found inside emotions, feelings, sometimes passion, or deep interest on the part of the author. In *Come On, Rain*, the themes are of neighborhoods and friendship. Notice how in our read-alouds each page contributes to a big idea." Read aloud *In the Fiddle Is a Song* by Durga Bernhard. "How does each page contribute to the writer's big idea?"

IP: "Work with a partner to explore texts in search of big ideas. Be sure to pause to talk. Mark the pages where you feel a strong sense of the big idea."

WU: Two student partnerships share a successful search for big ideas.

Day 4

FI: "Readers ask questions as they read to discover the big ideas in a text." Read aloud the nonfiction text *Owen & Mzee: The True Story of a Remarkable Friendship*. "We will post questions as we read. Does our sense of the big idea change as we read?"

IP: "Ask questions of your reading as you read today. See how the questions help you figure out what the big ideas are in this text."

WU: "Readers ask questions to discover meaning in text."

Identification Stage

Day 5

FI: "Readers make connections as they read, to develop ideas." Read aloud the poem "Poem" by Langston Hughes. "What does this poem remind you of? How does this connection help you think about what the big ideas are?"

IP: "Read some poems in your basket. Find one that you make a connection to. How does the connection help you see the idea the poet is presenting?"

WU: "Readers make connections to find meaning. Even across genres, we see evidence of big ideas in text. These three texts all had big ideas about friendship, but they were expressed in very different ways, and through narrative, poetry, and nonfiction."

Guided Practice Stage

Day 6

FI: "Today we are going to look for ideas, big ideas, that we are developing in our own writing. Bring your writing to this Focused Instruction time and let's look for where we have big ideas in our writing already. What is the feeling of our pieces?"

IP: "Read each other's pieces. Look for places where mood and feeling capture big ideas."

WU: "What did you notice in your friends' writing?"

Day 7

FI: "In my writing, I notice I have written about my family three times. Each time, there are some big ideas I am working on, about love and also about helping each other. Take some time today to look through your folders. Are there big ideas you write about a lot?"

IP: Students look at folders and continue with writing. "Mark places where big ideas repeat."

WU: Chart big ideas.

Commitment Stage

Day 8

FI: "Your pages, your pictures, and your words should reinforce your big ideas. Reread today to see if that is the case. If there is a part that does not seem to have anything to do with them, in any way, then it does not belong in this piece."

IP: "Do your pages reflect your big ideas?"

WU: "We develop big ideas by capturing emotion, expertise, or passion."

Day 9

FI: Share big ideas from student pieces. "How have you shown your big idea through your writing?"

IP: Students finish writing.

WU: Students reflect on how the big idea goes across many pages.

Day 10

FI: "We have learned that big ideas can come from emotions and feelings, but also from passions and questions.

We have learned that writers commit to big ideas by thinking about them on every page and in every line.

We have learned that writers have big ideas in all genres."

IP: Students return independent reading and/or independent writing.

WU: Students reflect on how they are thinking about the big idea as they return to their independent work.

CHAPTER 6

A Day in the Teaching of Reading and Writing

So far we have studied three ways of looking at time in our teaching: a continuum, a year, and a unit. Now we will take a close look at the key ingredient of time in The Complete 4 teacher's life: a day in the teaching of reading and writing.

The simplest way to think about a day and about how we integrate reading and writing instruction in such a way that your students (and you, too!) will find your day manageable is to think in terms of three containers for teaching and learning that are the *same* in both reading and writing instruction:

- Your reading and writing instruction begins with a whole-group Focused Instruction. This whole-group Focused Instruction lasts approximately 20 minutes. When you are paralleling reading and writing work, you need just one major Focused Instruction point, which connects to both reading and writing.

- Students engage in Independent Practice while you conduct small instructional groups or confer with individual students. Daily practice is an essential ingredient in The Complete 4 program. The length of time students can sustain their work independently or in small groups will vary across grades and years as students build stamina. However, as a general rule, you can expect to spend about 50 percent of your available time here.

- End your reading/writing time with a Wrap-Up. Students return to the meeting area, or simply reorient themselves back to the teacher. This time lasts approximately seven minutes. You will review and reflect on the day's work, using specific student examples in your reflection. Students will have an opportunity to ask questions if they need clarification of earlier instruction, or additional clarity going forward.

Focused Instruction

The Focused Instruction is your most explicit whole-group teaching time. You will present to your whole class, daily, brief teaching points using literature, student work, teacher work, student experience, and teacher experience as helpful supports. Your Focused Instruction does not exist in isolation. It is connected to the lessons that came before and the lesson that will come tomorrow. Units of study give you the opportunity to focus your instruction. I have identified four components to help you plan your Focused Instruction time: warm-up, teach, try, clarify.

Warm-Up

1. **Purpose:** To set the stage for teaching that will be shared in this lesson by connecting your students to your previous teaching points; to activate your students' prior knowledge of a subject; to focus or capture students' attention and interest.

2. **Methods for staging the warm-up:** Refer to yesterday's lesson; refer to an anchor chart; share an example/excerpt

from your own writing/reading experience; share an analogy that connects to the upcoming teaching point; share an example/excerpt from a student's reading/writing experience.

3. **Target language during the warm-up:** "Yesterday we learned . . ."; "For the past week we have been studying . . ."; "In this unit we are exploring . . ."

Teach

1. **Purpose:** To state your explicit teaching point; to demonstrate your teaching point by giving clear examples; to give students a succinct and explicit idea of what you expect from them— i.e., what you want them to do.

2. **Methods for teaching:** Read/write in front of your students, modeling your process and naming it; read aloud a portion of text that supports your teaching point, or display it in some way as a shared reading; role-play with a student to demonstrate a successful strategy; share a text (yours, your students', or published) that makes your teaching point; retell a conference you have had with a student in which he or she tried something new that you would like the whole class to try; be very, very explicit at this juncture, defining the exact task that you are setting out for your students.

3. **Target language for teaching:** "Today I will teach you . . ."; "Watch me as I . . ."; "Let's look together at . . . to find examples of . . ."; "I noticed [student's name] doing . . ."

Try

1. **Purpose:** To practice the skill/strategy with guidance; to assess students' understanding of the teaching point so that you can coach struggling students and plan additional conference time with them, and/or plan a small instructional group that will follow the Focused Instruction, perhaps for more than one day, to help you keep good track of those who are struggling.

2. **Methods:** Try this strategy/convention/genre element/process in your own reading/writing (for just four to five minutes);

turn and talk with a partner to restate what you have just learned; talk through your thinking; practice a strategy, convention, process with a partner; try the teaching as a shared-writing experience, creating a shared text to be used the next day; make a plan for your practice, using a sticky note or a notebook to record what you will do next.

3. **Target language:** "Now you are going to try this"; "Think about what I have just said, and practice this strategy with a partner beside you: think, turn, and talk"; "Take a few minutes to try this in your own writing while we are here together."

Clarify

1. **Purpose:** To connect your teaching point to ongoing Independent Practice.

2. **Method:** Restate your teaching point.

3. **Target language:** "When you are reading/writing today, I want you to . . ."; "Today we have learned . . . and we are going to . . . in our own reading/writing"; "You have been . . . in your Independent Practice time. When you go back to that today, continue thinking about . . ."; "Tomorrow we will . . ."; "When you return to your Independent Practice today, I will be looking for . . ."

Focused Instruction is connected to the work we are doing inside a unit; is connected to the work of the student readers and writers in your classroom; sometimes connects to your own reading and writing practice as a way for you to model your thinking for your students; is clear and concise, and may be repeated throughout the unit; connects to the Wrap-Up; connects to the Independent Practice. Your Focused Instruction may include literature, interviews, biographies, speeches, and quotations by readers and writers that are used to inspire your students, to help them understand great writers' and readers' processes, and to help them name the qualities of good writing.

Your own writing provides a model for your students as they watch. For example, if we are studying poetry and my students are searching for ideas to ignite their poetry, to share my own process with students, I could model using an image of my dog, Emmy, running in a field, as a way that I might start my poem based on a single image. I could say to them that using one image to get myself started in my writing is very helpful to me as a writer. Then I could share where my writing ideas come from. I could say, "I write about things I wonder about, I remember, I imagine, and I observe," and then demonstrate each of these through my own writing.

Your own reading life is demonstrated in front of your students. I might show my students how I preview text before I dig in, asking for other readers' opinions, looking at the jacket, the title, bringing what I know about the author's prior work to my reading. For example, I might say, "I am just about to begin Dave Eggers's new book, called *What Is the What*. I know his other books tend to be a combination of his own life and fiction, so I am anticipating his unique blend of two genres as I read this new one." Talk about your own reading process with your students. For example, I might say, "Reading longer texts feels harder for me right before I go to bed, so, at that time of the evening, I most often choose to read a poem or magazine article for its brevity, and then I can finish it before I doze off."

Student writing and reading experience. On my SMART Board or overhead projector, I put up work students bring to the Focused Instruction period that is an example of what we are studying, to show the different stages of student revision. Use the student as an example of someone whose strategies and processes are working well for him or her.

Independent Practice

Independent Practice is the heart of The Complete 4 system, and the heart-beat of any solid comprehensive reading and writing program. It is where you can monitor, observe, witness, participate in, and celebrate the successes and challenges of your work and the work of your children. It is deeply satisfying, because it is all about capturing the moment of the learning and using it to shape your teaching. It is also deeply satisfying because every single piece of the most current and solid research shows us that children must read and write to learn to read and write! It seems so obvious, and I smile even as I write, but it must be said! As teachers, because we are so responsible and put so much pressure on ourselves, we tend to create all kinds of incredibly complicated ways to teach reading and writing. In fact, the most obvious way to teach it is the best way: LET CHILDREN READ AND WRITE. That's what Independent Practice is, except that the added beauty of it is that you are there to coach, nurture, cheer, instruct, and empathize as students journey forward toward independence.

Students will leave the Focused Instruction fortified to begin or return to the work they are engaged in during Independent Practice. In The Complete 4 classroom, you will see students working alone, in partnerships, or in text or writing clubs. Students should always be asked to practice something you have taught each day, but the key is that it should be practiced with materials at their reading and writing levels. This includes books that match their reading levels, and paper that matches their writing levels. Sometimes students are practicing something for several days in a row (for example, studying character through inferencing) because you want to let their thinking ripen and their conversations grow (and I mean this for primary and upper-grade teachers). All students should be able to practice independently what you have taught, because they are reading and writing *at their independent levels*.

During Independent Practice, your role is to confer with your students individually and/or meet with small reading and writing groups, as well as to make sure your environment is conducive to harmonious and peaceful reading and writing experiences. That is a tall order! Remember, that is one reason why we incorporate process units into our year: so that instead of feeling overwhelmed by all the management and conversations we must have in order to get our reading and writing time up and running successfully, we build these conversations and focused teaching points into our yearlong curriculum. The role of the student is to engage with a text that is at the right level for that student, and to write in such a way that reflects his or her true independent level. During your conferences, be on the extreme lookout for students who are not matched correctly with their reading materials in terms of decoding, comprehension, fluency, *and* stamina. Support your students in choosing texts to read and to use as writing mentors. Your job here is to create a climate that encourages your students to engage with you in a conference, setting goals and actively reflecting on work. Independent Practice is essential so that students can apply process, skills, and strategies they are learning during the Focused Instruction time to their own reading levels and writing topics. This time also allows your children to engage in the social aspects of reading and writing in as authentic a manner as possible, and to see themselves as an integral part of a joyous, harmonious, productive reading and writing community.

In the Independent Practice portion of your reading/writing time, students have access to materials that support this work. They include a reader's notebook; a writer's notebook (these two may be combined); a text set that is chosen by student and teacher according to the student's reading level and interest; sticky notes and highlighters, paper clips, all the tools that help students stop and think as part of their reading and writing experience; drafting paper of different varieties—depending on the genre or audience, students may choose paper that suits the needs and goals of the writing outcome (for example, long, thin strips of paper for a poem, lined paper for a letter).

Before the conference/small-group meeting, review your notes on the student/ group; review the student's writing and the student's history as a reader; reflect on what you know about this reader/writer; set your goal for the conference/ small-group meeting.

During the conference: Connect with the student by sharing what you are noticing about his or her reading/writing progress; review work from the previous conference; refer to the reading/writing work of the unit; notice the qualities of good writing/reading the student is currently demonstrating; ask one focused question to gain further information about the student at the current time, such as "How is your writing going today?" or "Is this unit feeling productive for you as a reader/writer?" Move into teaching: Teach one point clearly and be explicit about the goals you have for the conference; connect the teaching point to the unit of study; engage the student in your teaching point by having him or her try some part of your teaching point in the conference; ask the student to restate the learning and practice the teaching point in his or her ongoing work. Give him the opportunity to ask you a question or to launch the conference with his own self-assessment and hopes for going forward. Assess, teach, try, and clarify in every conference.

During the small-group instruction, which may be guided reading or writing groups based on your knowledge of your students, cluster the students together appropriately. The groups are flexible, in that groupings will change across the year depending on the kind of work your students are doing and what their strengths and areas of need are. Remember to warm up, teach, try, and clarify, with a focus on deep, leveled teaching.

Warm-up in small-group instruction: "This week we have been working on. . ."; Teach: Depending on readiness of the group and the extent to which it is incorporating and understanding the prior teaching from the Focused Instruction periods, revisit past teaching or extend teaching. Try: Students will have the opportunity in the presence of the group to take a new try, or another try, at something that relates to the work of the unit or something that relates to the minor emphasis of the unit but with which they are still having trouble. Clarify: You are taking notes on the work of the group, looking at both individual progress and how the group interacts and works together. You will clarify the day's work, and either you or a group member will restate the day's teaching point.

The Wrap-Up

Whole-class focused discussion at the close of Independent Practice is no more than five to seven minutes in length. The purpose of the Wrap-Up is to bring closure to the day's work, set a plan for the coming days, and use specific examples to honor student effort during Independent Practice, as well as give children a chance to ask one last question or clarify an earlier point.

What it can look like: You can use student reading/writing to illustrate your teaching point from the day's work; two or three students think aloud about the day's/unit's work reflecting on their experience or sharing work from their Independent Practice; students try a new idea (two to three minutes), which you are introducing tomorrow in the Focused Instruction, that was generated during the Independent Practice time by another student; recount a conference or small-group teaching point; share your reactions, observations, and wonderings from your assessments during the Independent Practice time; students share their observations, reactions, and wonderings from the Independent Practice time; students share successes that relate specifically to the day's or the unit's major/minor teaching points; students share challenges encountered, and you set a time to work toward possible solutions; you leave the class with something specific to think about toward tomorrow's work.

Wherever I go, whenever I speak to groups of teachers, the longing in their eyes is always right there for answers to questions such as: But what do we do tomorrow? What is today's actual work? I understand this longing for the immediate kind of support, the today support, and this sense of urgency that accompanies that longing. The life of a teacher is intense, passionate, joyous, and sometimes frustrating, and sometimes all of that at the same time! It is hard to manage the big picture while still knowing you have six hours every day with a group of children with needs as diverse as the stars in the night sky. I would like to help you plan your daily instruction time in a way that will feel satisfying for you personally and help you live toward your biggest dreams as an educator. A well-designed lesson is genuinely empowering. Interestingly, the process and effort of designing the lesson ends up providing you with more of a chance to be spontaneous and responsive when you actually present the lesson to your class. Following my lessons or writing your own does not have to mean that you are following a "script." Like anything you want to do well, it is most helpful to break that task or skill into discreet parts and practice them before you put the whole together. I would like you to take a look at my sample lessons and then ask a colleague or two whom you really trust and feel comfortable with to write some together with you. The exercise of writing lessons may seem hard at first but may also be very exciting. You are reflecting on the craft of teaching: you are naming your teaching.

Let us take it one step at a time. Take a deep breath and plan backward. Use this book in your own teaching life to think: continuum, year, unit, and day. The day is an outgrowth of all that big thinking. It should *always* play toward your biggest ideas. When you plan, keep in mind:

- What happened yesterday

- What is going to happen tomorrow

- What outcomes I want for my students for the year, for the unit, and for today

Your classroom should reflect very visibly to a visitor the work you are doing in this Focused Instruction. When I walk into a Complete 4 classroom, I will see the following:

- Anchor charts reflecting the day's, week's, unit's learning, with headings such as: "Today we learned. . ." or "We are defining . . ." or "Effective readers . . ." or "Strong partners . . ." or "Our talk feels really great when . . ." or "Nonfiction is . . ." or "We notice commas when . . ."

- Student work: The walls and halls should reflect the work of your unit, but not just at the end of the unit! If you are interviewing family members for a nonfiction research unit, hang the interview notes. If you are collecting snippets of dialogue in your notebooks for a study of how to write fiction, hang sentence strips with dialogue samples. If you are studying collaboration in reading and writing, you might have walls posted with times when clubs are meeting, or book recommendations they are making to each other.

- Visible anchor texts: A Complete 4 unit is grounded in excellent texts, whether they are nonfiction articles or beautiful picture books or style guides for grammar reference. You may have a basket for these texts, from which students can browse, or you might even want to color-photocopy the text covers and hang them on the walls near the entrance to your room so everyone can see what texts are currently inspiring your community.

- Deadlines: A calendar that is easy to see and prominently
  featured is a good idea so your students can feel included in the
  planning process and help keep track of when projects are due.
  Mark your calendar with the project's due date at the beginning
  of a unit (so students and their parents can begin collecting
  materials at home in advance of the unit where applicable),
  at the midpoint of a unit, and then those that come at the end
  of a unit. Projects noted on the calendar can be as small as an
  index card with five favorite verbs to as large as a research
  project at the end of a longer unit.

Now I will share with you samples of Focused Instruction, with the parts
completely explained, so that you will feel comfortable creating your own. Also,
I will give you a sampling of what your Independent Practice and Wrap-Up
could look like if it were based on this Focused Instruction. The pieces are all
here for you; together they become The Complete 4 framework: balanced, yet
simple, with the structures for your design of these Focused Instructions being
exactly the same for both the teaching of reading and writing.

Unit of Study: Discovering Theme
Complete 4 Category: Strategy

Focused Instruction How does your thinking about your big idea change as you read?

Warm-Up

Connect previous teaching, capture students' attention and interest, and activate prior knowledge.	We have been talking about getting the big idea in books. The big idea is the main thing the book is about. Sometimes when we read we have an idea about what the book is about. Sometimes when we read, our idea changes as we read on.

Teach

Sustain one clear teaching point. DEMON-STRATE, using your work, anecdotes, students' work and anecdotes, and published work.	We have learned that the cover and title help us make a prediction about the big idea in a book. Sometimes, as we read on, the idea changes. We could read the first page and think the book is about one thing, and then as we read on, find out the book is about something more or something different.

Try

Engage students by asking them to turn and talk to a partner, envisioning how their work will go, or asking them to briefly try a reading or writing strategy together.	Model with partners in your class. Have them use an emergent book with a few words on each page. Partners will show the cover and make a prediction, then read the first page and see if their thinking has changed. Partners can then read the rest of the book to the class and discuss how their thinking about the big idea changed. Example of book title: *One Cold, Wet Night* by Joy Cowley

Clarify

Restate the teaching point and connect it to ongoing student work and outcomes in one or two sentences.	Today in your independent reading, choose a new book for your box. Your job is to read the title and make some guesses about the big idea. As you read on, see how your idea changes.

Independent Practice. In independent reading, students will choose a new book or text and practice making hunches about what they think the big idea (or theme) is going to be. They will talk with a partner about their hunches and even jot down thoughts on a sticky note if they can. Near the end of independent reading time, you will interrupt Independent Practice, asking students to confirm their hunches or revise them. In Independent Practice during writing time, you may want to have your students work with partners to have them get a hunch about what each other's big ideas are in their own writing. Students will also work on their own writing with an eye toward what their own big ideas are, perhaps even using sticky notes or highlighting places they think give hints about their big ideas or themes.

Wrap-Up. You may say to your students, "Today and this week we are practicing how we find the big idea in our reading and in our own writing. Today you had hunches about what the themes were in the books you are reading and in your partner's writing. We are going to chart some of our hunches today and take a look at this chart again tomorrow to see if our hunches are correct when we go back to our reading and writing. Tonight, when your mom or dad or babysitter is reading to you before you go to bed, be thinking about the themes in the books they are reading to you, and see if you notice any hints about what those themes are even before they begin. When you come in tomorrow, during our Focused Instruction time, we will talk a little bit about that, how you get hints about themes from everything from covers to titles to the first pages of books."

Unit of Study: Narrative
Complete 4 Category: Genre

Focused Instruction Strong Beginnings

Warm-Up	
Connect previous teaching, capture students' attention and interest, and activate prior knowledge.	Some writers start their books with questions, some with an opinion, some with a fact. All good beginnings get the reader's attention—you want your reader to be excited to read on!

Teach	
Sustain one clear teaching point. DEMON-STRATE, using your work, anecdotes, students' work and anecdotes, and published work.	Great beginnings get the reader's attention. They make the reader want to read on. A great beginning can have the following: • Noise words • Big letters • A question • Something funny • Something surprising • Words that make a picture in your mind [Teacher models a beginning he/she wrote to get the reader's attention.] <div align="center">Bat and Ball Day The crowds cheered! Hurray! Hurray! Hurray! The air smelled of popcorn, peanuts, hot dogs, hot pretzels and cotton candy. BAM! The bat hit the ball so hard it flew up, up, up, up, and out of the stadium!</div>

Try	
Engage students by asking them to turn and talk to a partner, envisioning how their work will go, or asking them to briefly try a reading or writing strategy together.	Turn and talk to the person next to you. Talk out loud about what you might try for your beginning to get the reader's attention.

Clarify	
Restate the teaching point and connect it to ongoing student work and outcomes in one or two sentences.	Today you are going to look at your pieces of writing and think about how to write a beginning to get the reader's attention. When you go back to your independent writing today, try at least one of the ways we talked about to make your beginning better. While you are writing, I will be looking for examples of places where you tried to make your beginning stronger.

Independent Practice. Students will use index cards to try out three different possible beginnings. They will choose their favorite and read it aloud to a partner.

Wrap-Up. You will review an anchor text, noticing the qualities of its good beginning, and adding the qualities to the anchor chart on what makes a great beginning. You will have selected one or two student samples to share aloud as well.

Unit of Study: Stamina
Complete 4 Category: Process

Focused Instruction Reading and Writing Long and Strong

Warm-Up

Connect previous teaching, capture students' attention and interest, and activate prior knowledge.	When I play tennis, I am learning skills so that I can play for longer periods of time and so it feels good when I play. The same is true for us as readers and writers. We learn skills to grow our "muscles" in reading and writing so we are strong and can go longer both in the amount we write and read, and in the amount of time we spend doing it. One thing that helps me in tennis is watching good players. When I watch good players, I ask myself, "What are they doing to become strong in their play?" I notice that they stretch between the breaks. I notice how they conserve their energy by using long strokes and getting their racket ready in position. These are the pointers I learn by watching.

Teach

Sustain one clear teaching point. DEMON-STRATE, using your work, anecdotes, students' work and anecdotes, and published work.	Today, I am going to show you some videotape of fifth grade readers and writers. In this tape you will see them in their independent work. I am going to ask you to watch the tape for clues about how they are becoming strong in their reading, how they are developing stamina.
	Notice their habits, their behaviors, and all the small things they might be doing when they get a little bit tired.

Try

Engage students by asking them to turn and talk to a partner, envisioning how their work will go, or asking them to briefly try a reading or writing strategy together.	Turn to your partner and discuss. What did you notice? What was working for these students? Together we will chart some of our findings: • The students take small breaks in the midst of their reading and writing. • The students turn and talk briefly when they come to a big idea in their reading and writing. • The students have found comfortable spots. • The students look as though they are reading something that is of high interest. • Some students are sitting alone, and some are sitting near a partner (readers and writers have different kinds of habits that work best for them).

Clarify

Restate the teaching point and connect it to ongoing student work and outcomes in one or two sentences.	Today, when you go to your reading and/or your writing, be thinking about all the ways readers and writers build their strength to stay long and strong with text. When we come back together, we will share what worked for us today, and we will star our chart for places where we tried what the fifth graders did.

Unit of Study: Punctuation
Complete 4 Category: Conventions

Focused Instruction Using the semicolon as a "super-comma" in detailed lists

Warm-Up

Connect previous teaching, capture students' attention and interest, and activate prior knowledge.	We've already discovered that the semicolon can be used to connect two related sentences. Writers will use the semicolon not because it is required, but because it makes the point they want to make. Usually they want us to know that the second part of the longer sentence is commenting on the first part. But that isn't the only reason to use a semicolon. Sometimes you'll see the semicolon used for a different reason. Let's look at this sentence from *The Van Gogh Café*. Listen and then consider—how and why does Cynthia Rylant use the semicolon in this example?

> . . . anyone who has ever visited the Van Gogh Café knows that magic comes from a building that was once a theater; from a sign above a cash register that reads BLESS ALL DOGS; from a smiling porcelain hen on top of a pie carousel; from purple hydrangeas painted all over a ladies' bathroom; from a small brown phonograph that plays "You'd Be So Nice to Come Home To."

If you look closely at the text between the semicolons, you'll see that these aren't separate sentences, but are dependent clauses. So why would the writer use semicolons here, rather than commas? How is this use of the semicolon different? Turn and talk to your neighbor about this question.

Teach

Sustain one clear teaching point. DEMON-STRATE using your work, anecdotes, students' work and anecdotes, and published work.	You've noticed that sometimes the semicolon can be used like a comma in a long list. Only here the list is full of lots of description, and the listed items are not individual words but lengthy clauses. In fact, the semicolon can be used like a super-comma, separating out elements in an elaborate list, so the reader knows exactly where one item in the list ends and another begins. You also noticed that the sentence began with commas, so if the author had continued to use the comma, the reader would possibly be confused by the author's message and intention. It doesn't happen often, but this is a great example of the semicolon as a super-comma in a long list.

Try	
Engage students by asking them to turn and talk to a partner, envisioning how their work will go, or asking them to briefly try a reading or writing strategy together.	Why do you think Cynthia Rylant constructed a sentence like this in the first chapter of her book? Turn and discuss this with a partner.

I listened in on one partnership with a theory that Cynthia Rylant has done this to provide us with a tantalizing preview of the chapters to come. If the Van Gogh Café is in fact magical, then each example cited in her long sentence and separated by semicolons will likely be the subject of future chapters. We will have to read ahead and see if they are right. |

Clarify	
Restate the teaching point and connect it to ongoing student work and outcomes in one or two sentences.	In your writing life today, I'd like you to try to use the semicolon. You may use it to join two related sentences together, where the second sentence comments on the first. Or you may try to use the semicolon as a super-comma in a long, detailed list. When our writing period ends, be prepared to share your sentence and the reason you chose to use a semicolon.

Independent Practice. Students will be writing in a variety of genres. They will use the semicolon in their writing today, marking the places where they used this mark, and preparing to share their thinking.

Wrap-Up. Students will come back together to share their attempt with a partner, and you will select two pairs to share why they chose to use the semicolon where they did and to demonstrate its usage.

In this book, we have explored a continuum, a year, a unit, and a day in the teaching of reading and writing. The increments of time for how we think about and consider our teaching can be made even smaller and smaller. If we zoom in on even a moment in time in our teaching, we would see worlds of ideas to think about and to discover in our own learning and our own professional growth. For each part of a lesson, the Focused Instruction is worth studying. Each day of Independent Practice is worth exploring. Each time our children come back together for the Wrap-Up is worth pondering. Each conference with each child is worth savoring and worth its own state of reflection. We are better teachers when we can continue to think of our teaching lives like those Russian dolls I mentioned at the beginning of this book, opening and opening and opening. Time should not be our enemy; let it instead be our container in which we situate our ideas and get better at our work. Time is our companion; our students are our companions, too, on these journeys. They are learning journeys for us all.

Teaching and Learning With Gratitude

At the beginning of this book, I thanked my teacher Mrs. Kovacs. If there is one thing I could leave you with at the end of this book, it would be about living a teaching life that is driven by gratitude. I have tried to remember that as I myself travel along a continuum, a year, my own self-created units of learning and growth, every single day. Sometimes gratitude is not easy; I have to practice it. Like anything, I get better with practice. Some days are better than others. But at the end of the day, I return to the questions that guide me: Do I feel complete? Am I complete with what I have done today, what I have done this year? I try to forgive myself for the work I have not yet done, and understand that being complete does not mean being finished or being perfect. It means I have done the best I can.

There is so much to be grateful for. I love the idea of teaching with gratitude, to be able to walk into a classroom and we turn around and say, What am I thankful for today? Is it Emma's perfect smile? Is it Jonah's funny way of ending each sentence like a question? Is it that I have found a way to learn something new today? Is it that Joe was able to read a complete page today?

Recently, I have talked to colleagues who are working worldwide to rebuild schools in postwar countries. I describe the way my colleagues and I build curriculum together by talking, thinking, planning, and implementing. I can see in their faces the longing they have for collegiality, for the opportunity to build together. And I realize that all of this, everything included in this book—the opportunity to do such things together: build a continuum, a year, a unit, and a lesson—is all a privilege.

Because it means we can come together. Because it means we can name what we teach, as it comes from our deepest longings and passions. When you sit around that table doing this work, my greatest wish for you is that you will find the potential for gratitude in it: appreciation for the coming together. In this way, together, we will become complete.

In my address book, I still have a piece of paper with the following names on it: Annora, Isabelle, Bert. I keep it there, and I look at it every so often. These were the names of my first students. I remember them with precious detail: Bert's laugh, and the day he cried with happiness because he read for the first time at the age of 11; Annora's beautiful long brown hair and her quick mind for poems; Isabelle's fluid grace on the basketball court, and my long trek to her apartment in Brooklyn to try to persuade her mother to let her try out for a more competitive team (she did not). I will never, ever get those kids out of my mind. They are part of who I am. They are part of my gratitude. Find your gratitude in your teaching. It is here you will feel most complete.

Every so often, I will be in a school and catch a glimpse of someone, and think, Oh, there's Bert, or Isabelle! A child, who, with a turn of the head, looks much like they did. And then I smile, realizing it has been years since they have been that age, and by now they are fully grown, living lives, I hope, of happiness.

Their continuum has continued, their years have come rushing by. I was there at a point along the way. I hope they remember me: part of their continuum, part of their own growing completeness. I hope they remember me the way I remember Mrs. Kovacs, with gratitude. That is how I remember them, for they were my teachers, too.

APPENDIX

The Complete 4™ Continuum Planner

Group Preparation

1. Select an initial strand for study. Use The Complete 4 categories to identify strands.

   Example: Poetry, Collaboration, Fluency, Interpretation

2. Individual teams or grade representatives outline their desired student outcomes within the strand. You may want to look to your state standards for implied articulation of skills within a strand.

Cross-Grade Conversation

3. Meet to share outcomes by grade. Seek consensus on how skills build across the grades.

   Example:

Grade	Strand: Nonfiction Reading
K	Why read nonfiction?
1	What is the difference between nonfiction and fiction?
2	Reading nonfiction in search of answers
3	Using text features and graphic aids effectively
4	Making inferences and drawing conclusions in nonfiction
5	Identifying and validating fact, opinion, and bias in nonfiction

4. Revisit existing teaching within the grade to refocus outcomes of unit, OR, use this new focus to write a unit of study within your grade.

The Complete 4™ Continuum Template

LitLife

Grade	Unit Focus	Framing Question	Performance Indicators	Anchor Texts
K				
1				
2				
3				
4				
5				

The Complete 4™ Yearlong Curriculum Planner

LitLife

Teacher: _____ Grade: _____ School: _____

Individual Preparation

1. Individually list desired student outcomes within each Complete 4 category.

2. Match outcomes to your state standards.

Process	✓ State Standard	Genre	✓ State Standard

Strategy	✓ State Standard	Conventions	✓ State Standard

Group Discussion

1. Identify performance indicators mentioned in state standards that you haven't listed in your own desired student outcomes.

_____

_____

_____

_____

_____

2. List other outcomes you strongly believe should be taught that aren't articulated in your state's standards.

_____

_____

_____

_____

_____

3. Seek consensus across your grade-level team in regard to student outcomes.

4. Look within Complete 4 categories to find outcomes that relate to one another. Here is an example.

Process	✓ State Standard
Talk well about books	
Consider other readers' perspectives	
Build independence	

5. Cluster these outcomes into a unit of study. Name the study to represent this thinking—for example, Book Partnerships or Book Clubs.

6. Continue to categorize your outcomes into units with a common objective. Look across The Complete 4 categories to name these units:

Process 30 percent	**Genre** 30 percent	**Strategy** 20 percent	**Conventions** 20 percent
• Creating a reading/ writing community (ARCH)	**Narrative:**	• Monitoring for meaning	• Concepts of print
• Reading/writing identity	• Fiction	• Rereading	• Word attack/word-solving skills
• Stamina	• Memoir	• Activating schema	• Grammar
• Pacing	• Personal essay	• Making connections	• End punctuation
• Fluency	• Short story	• Visualizing	• Pausing punctuation
• Conferring	• Play	• Determining importance	• Linking punctuation
• Peer conferring	• Folktales	• Inferring	• Dialogue
• Partnerships	• Mysteries	• Prereading (predictions, book walk, cover, blurb)	• Capitalization
• Text clubs	• Historical fiction		• Fluency and phrasing
• Text talk	• Fantasy	• Interpretation	• Syntax (sentence structure)
• Book choice	• Science fiction	• Critical analysis	• Sentence types/variety
• Making plans and setting goals	• Series	• Character analysis	• Parts of speech
• Storytelling	• Biography	• Story elements	• Editing
• Independence	**Persuasive Nonfiction:**	• Retelling	• Spelling strategies and resources
• Mentors	• Persuasive essay	• Summarizing	• Conventions as a craft tool
• Tools of a reader/writer	• Book blurbs/reviews	• Note-taking	• Paragraphs
• Content area reading/writing	• Literary essay/criticism	• Research	• Roots, prefixes, suffixes
• Writing about reading	• Editorial	• Theme study	• Word origins
• Assessment and reflection	• Debate	• Author study	
• Revision	• Speech	• Organizational structures	
• Writing under timed conditions	• Feature Article	• Revision	
• Finding writing ideas	**Informational Nonfiction:**	• Writing to a prompt	
• Developing writing ideas	• News article	• Studying craft strategies	
• The Four Prompts (Observe, Wonder, Remember, Imagine)	• Essay	• Close study of an anchor text	
• Techno-literacy	• Biography	• Reading like a writer	
	• All-about book		
	• How-to text		
	• Question/answer book		
	Poetry		
	Letters		
	Picture books		
	Standardized tests		

7. Make sure to balance your year with units across all four Complete 4 categories. LitLife suggests the following distribution of units across the year, although this can be *flexible*. Primary teachers may want to increase the percentage of process units slightly.

Process 30 percent

Genre 30 percent

Strategy 20 percent

Conventions 20 percent

Note: This distribution is based on number of units, not on overall time spent teaching the unit.

8. Place your units across the year, basing them on the following:

   - Key events

   - State testing

   - Curricular connections

9. Place your units across the year, looking to vary the type and length of unit, so students have a range of experiences. This brings an energy to student learning that does not happen when students are stuck in long units of the same purpose and type.

10: What does your year look like?

# of Weeks	Reading Unit	Complete 4 Category	Writing Unit	Complete 4 Category

Do you have a balance of units across The Complete 4?

Have you varied the type and length of units across the year?

Have you taken into consideration any key events (e.g., testing) in your timing of specific units?

Will these units hold all the teaching you feel is important to conduct across the year?

The Complete 4™ Reading and Writing Curriculum Calendar

LitLife

PROCESS=red
GENRE=green
STRATEGY=orange
CONVENTIONS=blue

Grade Level: _____

MONTH	READING UNITS	WRITING UNITS
Sept.		
Oct.		
Nov.		
Dec.		

MONTH	READING UNITS	WRITING UNITS
Jan.		
Feb.		
March		
April		
May		
June		

The Complete 4™ Unit-of-Study Planner

What are your desired outcomes for this unit?

_____

_____

_____

_____

Identify your major focus and minor focus (if there is one) for this unit.

Major	Minor

List two possible framing questions. Choose the one that feels most helpful in shaping the unit.

_____

_____

_____

_____

List three ways you will assess your students throughout this unit:

Assessment	Formal/Informal

What resources/texts/materials will you use?

Anchor Texts	Classroom Materials and Supplies

Imagine possible lessons within the stages of your study:

Stage of the Study	Anchor Language	Anchor Lessons
Immersion	Explore, Investigate, Notice, Discover, Reflect	
Identification	Name, Identify, Select, Determine	
Guided Practice	Find, Try, Experiment, Practice	
Commitment	Reflect, Celebrate, Connect, Plan, Commit, Assess...	

Establish a realistic time frame. How much time do you have budgeted for this unit? Will this timing match the planned instruction?

The Complete 4™ Unit-of-Study Template

Unit Major: _____ Length of Time: _____

Grade Level: _____ Unit Minor: _____

Complete 4 Major Category: _____

Complete 4 Minor Category: _____

Framing Question: _____

WEEK 1 IMMERSION/IDENTIFICATION

Day 1	Day 2	Day 3	Day 4	Day 5

WEEK 2 GUIDED PRACTICE

Day 1	Day 2	Day 3	Day 4	Day 5

WEEK 3 GUIDED PRACTICE

Day 1	Day 2	Day 3	Day 4	Day 5

WEEK 4 COMMITMENT

Day 1	Day 2	Day 3	Day 4	Day 5

Anchor Texts:

_____

_____

_____

_____

_____

_____

The Complete 4™ Lesson Planner

Unit of Study: _____ Lesson # _____

Stage of Unit: ☐ Immersion   ☐ Identification

☐ Guided Practice   ☐ Commitment

Name of Lesson: _____

What is the teaching that has preceded this lesson?

_____

_____

_____

How will you connect to ongoing learning?

- Anecdote _____
- Student work _____
- Quick summary _____

What prior knowledge will you need to activate?

_____

_____

How will you capture your students' interest?

- Anecdote _____
- Personal _____
- Class _____
- Individual _____

Your teaching point:

_____

_____

How will you demonstrate this?

☐ Modeled Think-Aloud   ☐ Instruct-Aloud   ☐ Student Work
☐ Your Own Writing   ☐ Shared Writing   ☐ Text
☐ Modeled Student Processes (conferences, public writing, talk)

How will students rehearse their learning before they begin their practice?

Turn and Talk: _____

_____ or Quick Try: _____

_____

What will your students do today during Independent Practice?

_____

_____

_____

What is their accountability during Independent Practice today?

_____

_____

_____

How will you assess your students during Independent Practice?

Product: _____

_____

Process: _____

_____

Will tomorrow's teaching:

- Connect to today's teaching? _____
- Shift to a new stage? _____
- Reflect on something that happened today? _____

How will this lesson connect to the larger goals of the unit?

_____

_____

_____

The Complete 4™ Lesson Template

Unit of Study: _____ Day # _____

Focused Instruction: _____

Warm-Up	
Connect previous teaching, capture students' attention and interest, and activate prior knowledge.	

Teach	
Sustain one clear teaching point. DEMONSTRATE using your work, anecdotes, students' work and anecdotes, and published work.	

Try	
Engage students by asking them to turn and talk to a partner, envisioning how their work will go, or asking them to briefly try a reading or writing strategy together.	

Clarify	
Restate the teaching point and connect it to ongoing student work and outcomes in one or two sentences.	

BIBLIOGRAPHY

Process

Anderson, C. (2000). *How's it going?: A practical guide to conferring with student writers.* Portsmouth, NH: Heinemann.

Atwell, N. (2005). *Naming the world: A year of poems and lessons.* Portsmouth, NH: Heinemann.

Buckner, A. (2005). *Notebook know-how.* Portland, ME: Stenhouse.

Calkins, L. (1994). *The art of teaching writing.* Portsmouth, NH: Heinemann.

Cruz, M. C. (2004). *Independent writing: One teacher—thirty-two needs, topics and plans.* Portsmouth, NH: Heinemann.

Davis, J., & Hill, S. (2003). *The no-nonsense guide to teaching writing.* Portsmouth, NH: Heinemann.

Giacobbe, M. E. (2007). *Talking, drawing, writing: Lessons for our youngest writers.* Portland, ME: Stenhouse.

Graham, P. (Ed.). (1999). *Speaking of journals: Children's book writers talk about their diaries, notebooks and sketchbooks.* Honesdale, PA: Boyds Mills.

Graves, D., & Kittle, P. (2005). *Inside writing: How to teach the details of craft.* Portsmouth, NH: Heinemann.

Harwayne, S. (1992). *Lasting impressions: Weaving literature into the writing workshop.* Portsmouth, NH: Heinemann.

Leograndis, D. (2006). *Fluent writing: How to teach the art of pacing.* Portsmouth, NH: Heinemann.

Murray, D. (2003). *A writer teaches writing* (2nd ed.). Belmont, CA: Heinle.

National Institute of Child Health and Human Development. (2002). *Report of the National Reading Panel. Teaching children to read: An evidence-based assessment of the scientific research literature on reading and its implications for reading instruction: Reports of the sub-groups* (NIH Publication No. 00-4754). Washington, DC: U.S. Government Printing Office. Also available online: http://www.nichd.nih.gov/publications/nrp/report.htm.

Opitz, M. (2007). *Don't speed. Read: 12 steps to smart and sensible fluency instruction.* New York, NY: Scholastic.

Rasinski, T. (2003). *The fluent reader: Oral reading strategies for building word recognition, fluency, and comprehension.* New York, NY: Scholastic Professional Books.

Ray, K. W. (2001). *The writing workshop: Working through the hard parts (and they're all hard parts).* Urbana, IL: NCTE.

Ray, K. W., & Cleaveland, L. B. (1999). *About the authors: Writing workshop with our youngest writers.* Portsmouth, NH: Heinemann.

Genre

Atwell, N. (2002). *Lessons that change writers.* Portsmouth, NH: Heinemann.

Bomer, R. (1995). *Time for meaning: Crafting literate lives in middle and high school.* Portsmouth, NH: Heinemann.

Duthie, C. (1996). *True stories: Nonfiction literacy in the primary classroom.* Portland, ME: Stenhouse.

Fountas, I., & Pinnell, G. S. (2006). *Teaching for comprehension and fluency: Thinking, talking, and writing about reading, K–8.* Portsmouth, NH: Heinemann.

Graves, D. (1989). *Experiment with fiction.* Portsmouth, NH: Heinemann.

Heard, G. (1989). *For the good of the earth and the sun: Teaching poetry.* Portsmouth, NH: Heinemann.

Heard, G. (1998). *Awakening the heart: Exploring poetry in elementary and middle school.* Portsmouth, NH: Heinemann.

Jorgensen, K. (2001). *The whole story: Crafting fiction in the upper elementary grades.* Portsmouth, NH: Heinemann.

Lattimer, H. (2003). *Thinking through genre: Units of study in reading and writing workshops 4–12.* Portland, ME: Stenhouse.

Parsons, S., & Ray, K. W. (2005). *First grade writers: Units of study to help children plan, organize, and structure their ideas.* Portsmouth, NH: Heinemann.

Stead, T. (2001). *Is that a fact?: Teaching nonfiction writing K–3.* Portland, ME: Stenhouse.

Wells, J., & Reid, J. (2004). *Writing anchors: Explicit lessons that identify criteria, offer strategic support, and lead to owner-ship of writing.* Portland, ME: Stenhouse.

Strategy

Fletcher, R. (1992). *What a writer needs.* Portsmouth, NH: Heinemann.

Fletcher, R., & Portalupi, J. (1998). *Craft lessons: Teaching writing K–8.* Portland, ME: Stenhouse.

Fletcher, R., & Portalupi, J. (2001). *Nonfiction craft writing lessons: Teaching information writing K–8.* Portland, ME: Stenhouse.

Fountas, I., & Pinnell, G. S. (2006). *Teaching for comprehension and fluency: Thinking, talking, and writing about reading, K–8.* Portsmouth, NH: Heinemann.

Harvey, S., & Goudvis, A. (2000). *Strategies that work: Teaching comprehension to enhance understanding.* Portland, ME: Stenhouse.

Heard, G. (2002). *The revision toolbox: Teaching techniques that work.* Portsmouth, NH: Heinemann.

Keene, E. O., & Zimmerman, S. (2007). *Mosaic of thought, second edition: The power of comprehension-strategy instruction.* Portsmouth, NH: Heinemann.

Laminack, L. (2006). *Learning under the influence of language and literature: Making the most of read-alouds across the day.* Portsmouth, NH: Heinemann.

Le Guin, U. K. (1998). *Steering the craft: Exercises and discussions on story writing for the lone navigator or the mutinous crew.* Portland, OR: Eighth Mountain Press.

Miller, D. (2002). *Reading with meaning: Teaching comprehension in the primary grades.* Portland, ME: Stenhouse.

Pearson, P. D., & Taylor, B. M. (Eds.). (2002). *Teaching reading: Effective schools, accomplished teachers.* Mahwah, NJ: Lawrence Erlbaum.

Pressley, M. (2005). *Reading instruction that works: The case for balanced teaching* (3rd ed.). New York, NY: Guilford.

Ray, K. W. (1999). *Wondrous words: Writers and writing in the elementary classroom.* Urbana, IL: NCTE.

Conventions

Anderson, J. (2005). *Mechanically inclined: Building grammar, usage, and style into writer's workshop.* Portland, ME: Stenhouse.

Angelillo, J. (2002). *A fresh approach to teaching punctuation.* New York, NY: Scholastic.

Atwell, N. (2002). *Lessons that change writers.* Portsmouth, NH: Heinemann.

Ehrenworth, M., & Vinton, V. (2005). *The power of grammar: Unconventional approaches to the conventions of language.* Portsmouth, NH: Heinemann.

O'Conner, P. T. (2001). *Woe is I.* Minneapolis, MN: Tandem Library Books.

Shertzer, M. (1996). *The elements of grammar.* New York, NY: Longman.

Snowball, D., & Bolton, F. (1999). *Teaching spelling K–8: Planning and teaching.* Portland, ME: Stenhouse.

Stilman, A. (2004). *Grammatically correct: The writers essential guide to punctuation, spelling, style, usage and more.* Cincinnati, OH: F & W Publications.

Strunk, W., Jr., & White, E. B. (1999). *The elements of style* (4th ed.). New York, NY: Longman.

Truss, L. (2004). *Eats, shoots & leaves: The zero tolerance approach to punctuation.* New York, NY: Gotham Press.

Weaver, C. (1996). *Teaching grammar in context.* Portsmouth, NH: Heinemann.

Wilde, S. (2007). *Spelling strategies and patterns: What kids need to know.* Portsmouth, NH: Heinemann.

Focused Instruction

Allington, R. (2002). *Reading to learn: Lessons from exemplary fourth-grade classrooms.* New York, NY: Guilford.

Day, J. P., Spiegel, D. L., McLellan, J., & Brown, V. B. (2002). *Moving forward with literature circles: How to plan, manage, and evaluate literature circles that deepen understanding and foster a love of reading.* New York, NY: Scholastic.

Gallagher, K. (2004). *Deeper reading: Comprehending challenging texts, 4–12.* Portland, ME: Stenhouse.

Smith, F. (2004). *Understanding reading* (4th ed.). New York, NY: Lawrence Erlbaum.

Wells, J., & Hart-Hewins, L. (1999). *Better books! Better readers!: How to choose, use and level books for children in the primary grades.* Portland, ME: Stenhouse.

English Language Learners

Del Vecchio, A., & Guerrero, M. (1995). *Handbook of English language proficiency tests.* Albuquerque, NM: Evaluation Assistance Center, Western Region, New Mexico Highlands University.

Fillmore, L. W., & Snow, C. (2000). *What teachers need to know about language.* Washington, DC: Center for Applied Linguistics.

Freeman, D., & Freeman Y. (2007). *English language learners: The essential guide.* New York, NY: Scholastic.

García, G. G., & Beltrán, D. (2003). *Revisioning the blueprint: Building for academic success of English learners.* Newark, DE: International Reading Association.

Helman, L. (2005). Using literacy assessment results to improve teaching for English-language learners. *The Reading Teacher, 58*(7), 668–677.

Krashen, S. (2003). *Explorations in language acquisition and use.* Portsmouth, NH: Heinemann.

Krashen, S. (2004). *The power of reading: Insights from the research* (2nd ed.). Portsmouth, NH: Heinemann.

INDEX